My
LinkedIn®

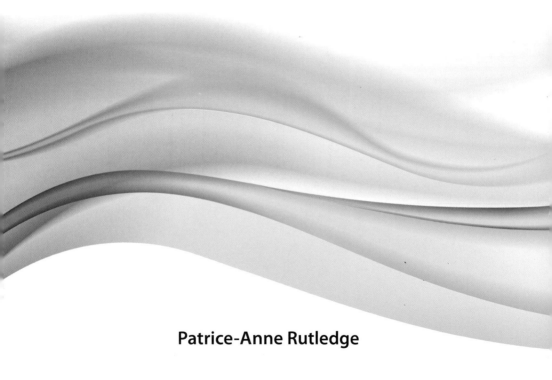

Patrice-Anne Rutledge

que®

800 East 96th Street,
Indianapolis, Indiana 46240 USA

My LinkedIn

Copyright © 2014 by Pearson Education, Inc.

ISBN-13: 978-0-7897-5270-3

ISBN-10: 0-7897-5270-0

Library of Congress Control Number: 2013956990

Printed in the United States of America

First Printing: December 2013

Trademarks

All terms mentioned in this book that are known to be trademarks or service marks have been appropriately capitalized. Que Publishing cannot attest to the accuracy of this information. Use of a term in this book should not be regarded as affecting the validity of any trademark or service mark.

Warning and Disclaimer

Every effort has been made to make this book as complete and as accurate as possible, but no warranty or fitness is implied. The information provided is on an "as is" basis. The author and the publisher shall have neither liability nor responsibility to any person or entity with respect to any loss or damages arising from the information contained in this book or from the use of the CD or programs accompanying it.

Special Sales

For information about buying this title in bulk quantities, or for special sales opportunities (which may include electronic versions; custom cover designs; and content particular to your business, training goals, marketing focus, or branding interests), please contact our corporate sales department at corpsales@pearsoned.com or (800) 382-3419.

For government sales inquiries, please contact governmentsales@pearsoned.com.

For questions about sales outside the U.S., please contact international@pearsoned.com.

Editor-in-Chief
Greg Wiegand

Senior Acquisitions Editor
Michelle Newcomb

Development Editor
Charlotte Kughen

Managing Editor
Sandra Schroeder

Project Editor
Seth Kerney

Copy Editor
Karen Gill

Indexer
Angie Bess Martin

Proofreader
Jess DeGabriele

Technical Editor
Vince Averello

Editorial Assistant
Cindy Teeters

Book Designer
Mark Shirar

Compositor
Mary Sudul

Contents at a Glance

Table of Contents

vi

11 Working with LinkedIn Recommendations   199

12 Working with LinkedIn Endorsements   219

About the Author

Patrice-Anne Rutledge is a business technology author and journalist who writes about social media, web-based applications, and small business technology. Patrice is a long-time LinkedIn member and social networking advocate who uses LinkedIn to develop her business, find clients, recruit staff, and much more.

My LinkedIn is Patrice's fifth book about LinkedIn. She is also the author of *LinkedIn Essentials*, a video training series from Pearson Education. Her other books include *WordPress on Demand*, *Office 2013 All-In-One Absolute Beginner's Guide*, *Sams Teach Yourself Google+ in 10 Minutes*, *Using Facebook*, and *The Truth About Profiting from Social Networking*, all from Pearson. She is also the author of *LinkedIn Essentials*, a video training series. She can be reached through her website at www.patricerutledge.com.

Dedication

To my family, with thanks for their ongoing support and encouragement.

Acknowledgments

Special thanks to Michelle Newcomb, Charlotte Kughen, Vince Averello, Seth Kerney, and Karen Gill for their feedback, suggestions, and attention to detail.

We Want to Hear from You!

As the reader of this book, *you* are our most important critic and commentator. We value your opinion and want to know what we're doing right, what we could do better, what areas you'd like to see us publish in, and any other words of wisdom you're willing to pass our way.

We welcome your comments. You can email or write to let us know what you did or didn't like about this book—as well as what we can do to make our books better.

Please note that we cannot help you with technical problems related to the topic of this book.

When you write, please be sure to include this book's title and author as well as your name and email address. We will carefully review your comments and share them with the author and editors who worked on the book.

Email: feedback@quepublishing.com

Mail: Que Publishing
         ATTN: Reader Feedback
         800 East 96th Street
         Indianapolis, IN 46240 USA

Reader Services

Visit our website and register this book at quepublishing.com/register for convenient access to any updates, downloads, or errata that might be available for this book.

LinkedIn home page

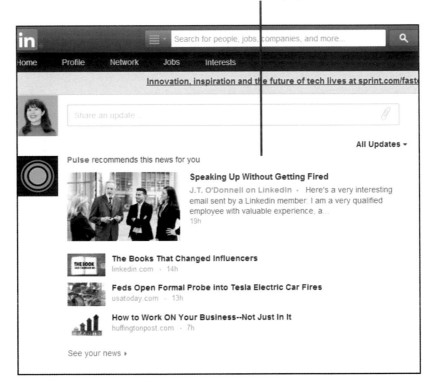

In this prologue, you learn about LinkedIn—the leading professional networking site on the Web:

→ Exploring what you can do with LinkedIn
→ Discovering what makes LinkedIn different
→ Understanding the key to LinkedIn success

Getting to Know LinkedIn

LinkedIn (www.linkedin.com) is the world's leading social networking site for business, with profiles of hundreds of millions of professionals around the world. LinkedIn is also rapidly expanding: Two new members join approximately every second. The site is extremely active with recruiters from recruiting firms as well as from major companies such as Microsoft, eBay, Sony, Walmart, and PepsiCo, which makes it a prime hunting ground for job seekers. Everyone from top CEOs to President Barack Obama has a LinkedIn profile. If you want to network for business on just one social networking site, LinkedIn is the site to choose.

Understanding What You Can Do with LinkedIn

Creating a professional profile and developing a solid network of connections on LinkedIn can help you meet many goals. For example, participation on LinkedIn can enable you to do the following:

- Find a job or recruit quality job candidates

- Brand yourself online with a professional presence that demonstrates your expertise

- Develop your business by creating a Company Page and connecting with potential clients and partners

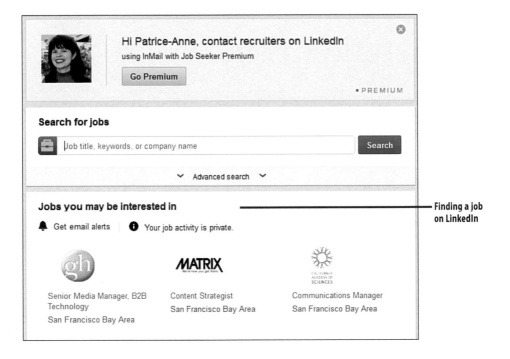

Finding a job on LinkedIn

LinkedIn Company Page

LinkedIn History

LinkedIn was established in May 2003 when the five company founders invited 350 of their closest business contacts to join. By the end of that first year, LinkedIn had reached 81,000 members.

Discovering What Makes LinkedIn Different

It's clear that today's technology has forever changed the way people find a job, promote their businesses, foster strategic partnerships, and develop their professional networks. But technology is just the enabler. The fundamental concepts of professional networking remain the same both online and off. Building relationships through mutual connections and trust is the foundation of networking on LinkedIn, just as it is in the real world.

Focus on Strategy, Not Filling Out Forms

At first glance, LinkedIn appears deceptively simple. Its true power, however, comes from employing the strategic best practices of online networking, not on your ability to enter your professional data in a form.

Before getting started with LinkedIn, however, you need to understand its unwritten rules that distinguish it from other social networking sites. LinkedIn's focus is on developing a mutually beneficial online business network. With LinkedIn, you can stay in touch with your existing contacts and connect with other professionals who share your goals and interests. LinkedIn is not the place to amass thousands of "followers," engage in heavy sales tactics, or send spam-like communications. Keeping these rules in mind can help you develop a LinkedIn strategy that generates positive results in your professional career.

Understanding the Key to LinkedIn Success

The key to success on LinkedIn is to establish clear goals and ensure that all your actions on the site work to achieve those goals.

For example, if your goal is to find a job on LinkedIn, you want to create a strong profile with keywords that attract recruiters. You also want to develop a solid network of professional contacts in your industry—the type of people who might hire you or who might provide relevant job leads.

On the other hand, if your goal is to find business leads and develop your platform as an expert in your field, you could use a different approach. A strong profile and network of connections are still important, but you might also want to post informative status updates and participate in LinkedIn Groups to promote your expertise among LinkedIn's millions of members.

My LinkedIn is designed to get you up and running on LinkedIn as quickly as possible. This book focuses on standard LinkedIn functionality. LinkedIn rolls out beta functionality and new features on a regular basis, so the features available to you might vary at any given time. For now, turn to Chapter 1, "Creating Your LinkedIn Account," to get started with this powerful networking tool.

LinkedIn
home
page

Navigation
bar

Share
updates

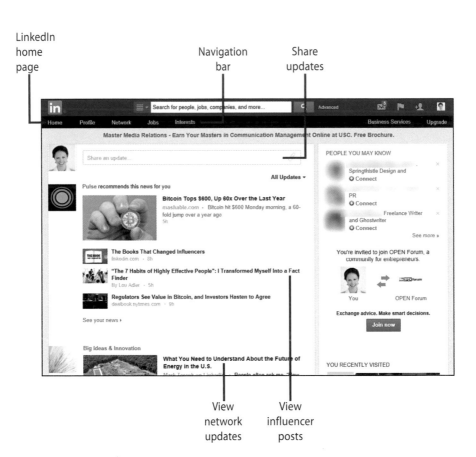

View
network
updates

View
influencer
posts

In this chapter, you learn how to sign up for a LinkedIn account, navigate LinkedIn, choose the right LinkedIn account for your goals, and get familiar with the LinkedIn site. Topics in this chapter include:

→ Creating a LinkedIn account
→ Exploring the LinkedIn home page
→ Navigating LinkedIn
→ Signing in to LinkedIn
→ Signing out of LinkedIn
→ Viewing the LinkedIn blog
→ Getting help
→ Upgrading to a LinkedIn premium account

1

Creating Your LinkedIn Account

Creating an account on LinkedIn, the world's most popular professional networking site, is easy. Best of all, its basic features are all free.

Getting Started with LinkedIn

Signing up for a LinkedIn account is a simple, straightforward task.

Create a LinkedIn Account

You can quickly create a basic site on LinkedIn (www.linkedin.com).

1. Enter your first name, last name, email address, and a password.

2. Click the Join Now button.

Create a Strong Password

A password that contains a combination of uppercase and lowercase letters, numbers, and symbols provides the most protection.

Choose the Right Email Address

LinkedIn offers privacy controls to protect your business email address. Entering the email address that most of your business contacts use to communicate with you yields the best results when others try to connect with you by email on LinkedIn.

3. Select your country.

4. Enter your ZIP Code or postal code, depending on your choice of country.

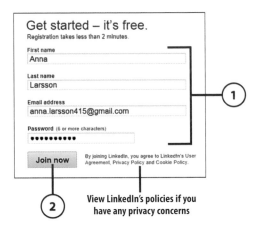

Get started – it's free.
Registration takes less than 2 minutes.

First name
Anna

Last name
Larsson

Email address
anna.larsson415@gmail.com

Password (6 or more characters)
••••••••••

Join now   By joining LinkedIn, you agree to LinkedIn's User Agreement, Privacy Policy and Cookie Policy.

View LinkedIn's policies if you have any privacy concerns

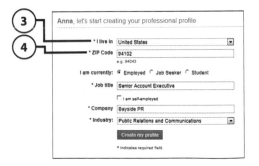

Anna, let's start creating your professional profile

* I live in   United States

* ZIP Code   94102
e.g. 94043

I am currently: ⦿ Employed ○ Job Seeker ○ Student

* Job title   Senior Account Executive

☐ I am self-employed

* Company   Bayside PR

* Industry   Public Relations and Communications

Create my profile

* indicates required field.

5. Select your employment status from the options available: Employed, Job Seeker, or Student.

Your Employment Status Controls Other Fields

The selection you make in employment status field affects which additional fields display on this page. This task displays fields for someone who is employed.

6. Enter your job title.

7. Enter your company. If LinkedIn doesn't find an existing match for the company you enter, the Industry field appears.

Anna, let's start creating your professional profile

* I live in United States
* ZIP Code 94102
            e.g. 94043
I am currently: ⦿ Employed ○ Job Seeker ○ Student
* Job title Senior Account Executive
            ☐ I am self-employed
* Company Bayside PR
* Industry: Public Relations and Communications
            Create my profile
* Indicates required field.

Let LinkedIn Find Your Company

As you start typing, LinkedIn locates potential company matches from existing profiles. Choosing from an existing entry helps ensure that you and your colleagues are correctly linked by company.

8. Select the industry that best describes your professional expertise from a list of more than 100 options.

Industry Options

Options in the Industry field range from popular professions (fields include Accounting, Banking, Computer Software, Internet, Real Estate, and Marketing and Advertising) to the more obscure (fields include Dairy, Gambling & Casinos, Fishery, and Think Tanks).

9. Click the Create My Profile button.

10. Click Skip This Step to bypass growing your network for now.

Complete Your Profile Before Connecting

At this stage, LinkedIn prompts you to search for and connect with people you know. However, I recommend you create your profile before completing this step. Why? Because when your contacts receive your connection request, you want them to view a complete profile, not an empty one.

11. Confirm your email address. What displays on this page varies based on the email provider you use. Complete the verification process based on the prompts LinkedIn provides you.

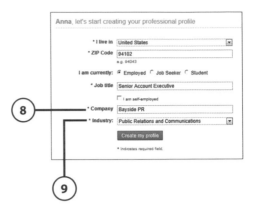

Understand the Email Verification Process

As a security measure, LinkedIn needs to verify the email address you entered when you signed up for an account. This ensures that the person who actually owns an email account, and not an impostor, signed up for LinkedIn.

12. Click Skip This Step to bypass notifying your social media contacts now.

Complete Your Profile Before Sharing

LinkedIn prompts you to let your Facebook friends and Twitter followers know that you just joined LinkedIn. Again, it's best to skip this step and inform your social media contacts after you create your profile.

13. Click the Basic Account button to start with a free LinkedIn account.

Start with a Free Account

Optionally, you can upgrade to a premium account immediately. Unless you're certain that you need the features offered with a premium account, however, it's a good idea to start with the free account.

14. LinkedIn displays your blank profile. You can enter data now or finish it later. See Chapter 2, "Creating Your LinkedIn Profile," for more information about creating a quality profile that gets results.

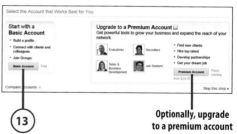

Optionally, upgrade to a premium account

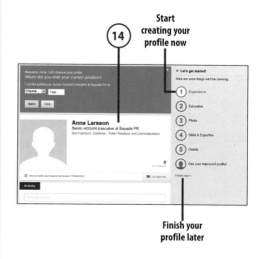

Start creating your profile now

Finish your profile later

Finding Your Way Around LinkedIn

LinkedIn includes millions of pages of data, so knowing how to find your way around can help save you lots of time. Fortunately, after you understand the LinkedIn navigation structure and the best ways to use your home page (command central on LinkedIn), you should be able to quickly find what you're looking for.

Explore the LinkedIn Home Page

When you first create a LinkedIn account, your home page displays minimal content, which is understandable considering that you don't have any contacts yet. A welcome box greets you, encouraging you to expand your network and start following people and companies. I recommend, however, that you create your profile before networking and following.

**When you're new, your
home page is rather empty**

It's important to remember the content on your home page is dynamic and is unique to your LinkedIn actions, network, and account settings. Your home page changes, however, as you start participating on LinkedIn. As an active LinkedIn user, the left column of your home page includes the following content:

Share your status

- Your current status and a text box for updating your status. See Chapter 5, "Managing and Updating Your Profile," for more information about updates.

• LinkedIn Pulse headlines, displaying relevant news articles as well as posts by LinkedIn influencers. See Chapter 9, "Viewing News on LinkedIn," for more information about LinkedIn Pulse and influencer posts.

• The latest updates from your network. By default, this section displays all updates, but you can narrow this to display only updates from your connections, articles people have shared, updates from group members, profile updates, and so forth. You can also search updates by keyword and specify which updates display on your home page. See Chapter 4, "Customizing Your LinkedIn Settings," for more information about customization options.

The right column of your home page displays the following:

• A list of three people you might know based on your existing connections. You can click the Connect link below a name to send an invitation to connect. If you haven't added any connections yet on LinkedIn, this option doesn't appear.

• A box with advertisements.

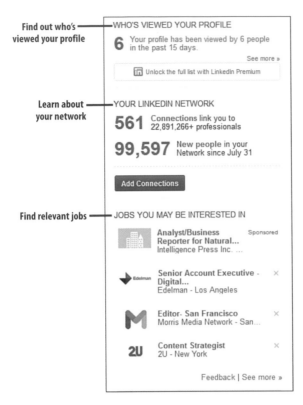

Find out who's viewed your profile

Learn about your network

Find relevant jobs

- The Who's Viewed Your Profile box, which tells you how many people have viewed your profile recently. To access details about who has viewed your profile, you must either allow others to view your name and headline when you visit their profiles or upgrade to a premium account. If you haven't created a profile yet or no one has viewed your profile, this option doesn't appear.

- The Your LinkedIn Network box lists your number of connections, the total size of your network, and the number of new people in your network.

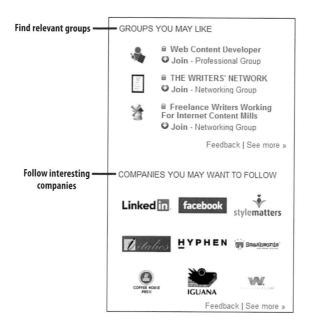

Find relevant groups ———

Follow interesting ———
companies

- Boxes for jobs, groups, and companies relevant to your background. LinkedIn uses the information from your profile to determine relevant content to display. For example, if you select Marketing as your industry, the content displayed should be useful to a marketing professional.

Navigate LinkedIn

Navigating LinkedIn is a straightforward process after you understand its navigational structure. LinkedIn pages display two navigation tools: a navigation bar at the top of the screen with two rows and a bottom menu of additional options.

The navigation bar includes links to the most popular LinkedIn destinations, with drop-down menus offering additional options.

Links on the top navigation menu include the following:

- **Home**—Return to the LinkedIn home page.

- **Profile**—Edit or view your profile and recommendations.

- **Network**—View contacts, add connections, and find alumni.

- **Jobs**—Perform an advanced job search or manage job postings.

- **Groups**—View your groups, view a group directory, or create a group.

- **Interests**—View and add companies, participate in groups, and follow influencers.

- **Business Services**—Post a job, access LinkedIn Talent Solutions (for recruiters), or create an ad.

- **Upgrade**—Purchase a premium account.

Help Center	About	Press	Blog	Careers	Advertising	Talent Solutions	Tools	Mobile	Developers	Publishers	Language

Upgrade Your Account

LinkedIn Corporation © 2013	User Agreement	Privacy Policy	Community Guidelines	Cookie Policy	Copyright Policy	Send Feedback

More options are available on the bottom menu

The bottom of the LinkedIn screen provides links to additional menu options, including LinkedIn company information, LinkedIn tools, and premium features.

Sign In to LinkedIn

After creating a LinkedIn account, you can sign in at any time at www.linkedin.com.

1. Enter your email address.
2. Enter your password.
3. Click the Sign In button.

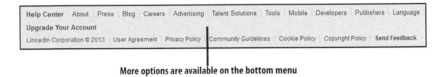

Need a New Password?
If you forget your password, you can click the Forgot Your Password link to reset it.

Sign Out of LinkedIn

If you're using LinkedIn on a public computer or a computer that other people have access to, you should sign out of your account when you're finished. Otherwise, you might stay signed in.

1. Pause your mouse over your photo.

2. Click the Sign Out link.

View the LinkedIn Blog

The LinkedIn blog offers useful advice on making the most of LinkedIn and also alerts you to changes and new features.

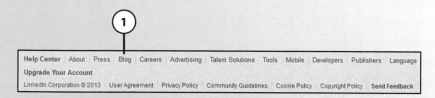

1. Click the Blog link on the bottom navigation menu.

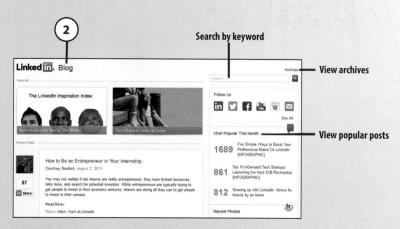

2. View the LinkedIn blog.

Get Help

If you need help with doing something on LinkedIn, particularly a new feature not covered in this book, you can access online help.

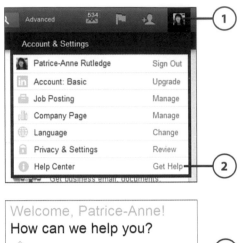

1. Pause your mouse over your photo.

2. Click the Get Help link.

3. Enter the help topic you want to see.

4. Click the Search button.

Choosing the Right LinkedIn Account Type

When you first sign up for LinkedIn, you receive a free basic account by default. This account offers so many powerful features that it should suit the needs of most users. Unless you specifically need a premium feature, try out the free account before making the decision to upgrade. With a free basic account, you can request a maximum of five introductions at one time, view 100 results per search, and save a maximum of three searches with weekly email alerts.

If you need more powerful networking features, you can upgrade to a paid premium account.

The LinkedIn Premium page offers four tabs with premium account options:

- LinkedIn Premium

- For Recruiters

- For Job Seekers

- For Sales Professionals

Within each type, LinkedIn offers three levels with increasing features and pricing. If you aren't a recruiter, job seeker, or sales professional, LinkedIn Premium offers a general selection of premium features.

>>>Go Further

EXPLORING LINKEDIN PREMIUM ACCOUNTS

Premium accounts offer you the ability to contact more people who aren't connected to you and are ideally suited to people using LinkedIn as a business development tool.

LinkedIn's premium accounts enable you to

- Receive an OpenLink Network membership

- Send unlimited OpenLink messages

- Access the complete list of who has viewed your profile

- View expanded profiles of everyone on LinkedIn—even people outside your network

- Perform unlimited one-click reference searches

- Receive LinkedIn customer service responses within one business day

Your choice of the specific premium account that's right for you depends on your needs for InMail, introductions, and searches.

>>>Go Further

UNDERSTANDING LINKEDIN TERMINOLOGY

LinkedIn uses unique terminology for some of its features. Here are some terms you need to know before evaluating and selecting a premium account:

- **InMail**—An InMail is a private message from a LinkedIn member who is not your connection. Although you can receive InMail free if you indicate that you are open to receiving InMail messages, you cannot send InMail unless you pay for that particular service. InMail is a paid service because messages you send via InMail are far less likely to be confused for spam. Keep in mind, however, that InMail isn't the same as the free messages you are able to exchange with people after you have already made a connection.

- **Introduction**—A LinkedIn introduction provides a way to reach out to people who are connected to your connections. By requesting an introduction through someone you already know, that person can introduce you to the person you're trying to reach. For example, one of your connections might be connected to a hiring manager at a company you want to work for. Requesting an introduction to this hiring manager is a much better way to find a job than just sending a resume along with hundreds of other people.

- **OpenLink Network**—The OpenLink Network is a LinkedIn premium feature that enables network members to contact each other without incurring additional fees.

Upgrade to a LinkedIn Premium Account

If you decide to upgrade to a paid account, you can do so in a few quick steps.

1. Click the Upgrade link.

2. Click the tab for the type of premium account you want. LinkedIn Premium is the default, but you can also choose For Recruiters, For Job Seekers, or For Sales Professionals.

3. Click the Annual option to pay upfront for a full year.

4. Click the Monthly link to be billed for your premium account each month.

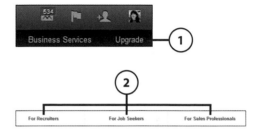

Get a Discount by Signing Up for an Annual Plan

If you sign up for an annual plan, you receive a substantial discount—up to 25% per year. Before choosing this option, however, it's a good idea to test a premium account for a month to verify it's the right option for you.

5. Review what's included in each plan in the Compare Plans section. For example, the higher priced plans include more InMail messages, introductions, searches, and so forth.

Do I Have to Sign Up for the Basic Plan?

The first column of the Compare Plans section displays the options available with the LinkedIn Basic plan. This is the default plan you receive when you sign up for LinkedIn. To keep this plan, you don't need to do anything.

6. Click the Start Now button below your preferred plan.

7. Enter your payment information including credit card details and your address.

8. Click the Review Order button to review your information and confirm your purchase.

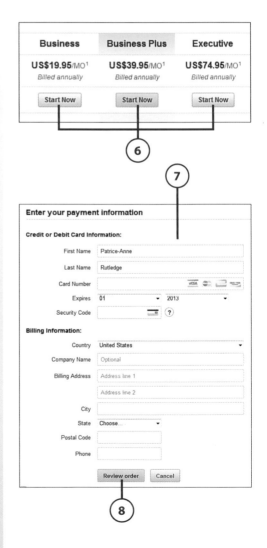

A complete LinkedIn profile

Patrice-Anne Rutledge

Digital Marketing Strategist at Pacific Ridge Media |
Business Technology Author

San Francisco Bay Area | Marketing and Advertising

Current	Pacific Ridge Media, Pearson Education
Previous	Oracle
Education	University of California, Irvine

Send Patrice-Anne InMail ▾

500+
connections

www.linkedin.com/in/patriceannerutledge

📇 Contact Info

Background

 Summary

◆ DIGITAL MARKETING STRATEGIST ◆

I'm the founder and principal of Pacific Ridge Media, a boutique digital agency specializing in social media, content marketing, and online branding.

In this chapter, you discover how to create a quality profile that matches your LinkedIn goals, including:

→ Exploring LinkedIn profiles

→ Editing basic profile information

→ Adding a photo

→ Adding a profile summary

→ Entering job and educational information

→ Attaching media files

→ Customizing your public profile and URL

2

Creating Your LinkedIn Profile

Profiles form the foundation of LinkedIn. Your profile is your LinkedIn calling card, providing a quick snapshot of your professional background and experience. Although creating a profile is straightforward, it's important that you choose the right profile content because it has a major impact on the success you achieve on LinkedIn.

Exploring LinkedIn Profiles

Before creating your own profile, it's a good idea to view a variety of member profiles to get an idea of what makes a quality profile. Although you should focus on viewing the profiles of others in your field (in other words, a little "competitive intelligence"), also take the time to explore profiles of professionals in other fields and geographic regions.

A profile can include the following:

- A summary of your professional experience and specialties

- Your photo

- Your status with comments from your network

- A list of the positions you've held and your major accomplishments at each

- A list of the educational institutions you've attended and your major accomplishments at each

- Sections where you can list certifications, courses, test scores, publications, awards, patents, volunteer experience, languages you speak, and specific skills you have

- Professional recommendations and endorsements

- Media files such as documents, videos, presentations, or images

- A list of your LinkedIn connections

- Information about your interests, association memberships, honors, and awards

- Your contact settings

- A list of your opportunity preferences

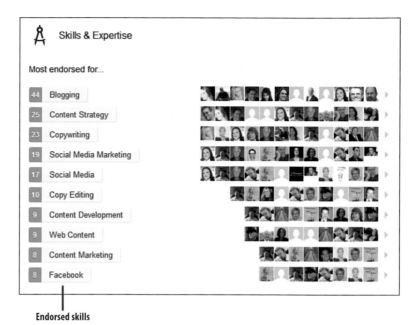

Endorsed skills

Account Executive

Tipford PR

2005 – 2007 (2 years)

Assisted with media relations and social media for several high-profile lifestyle clients. Wrote press releases and other press materials. Pitched stories and secured media coverage.

▾ 1 recommendation

 Sara Wretstrom
Account Manager at Tipford PR

Felice worked for me for two years at Tipford PR. She's an excellent writer with solid social media and media relations skills who also a polished and poised presenter. I would welcome the opportunity to work with Felice again. View ↓

Position with
recommendation

>>>Go Further

CREATING A PROFILE THAT ACHIEVES YOUR GOALS

Before you create your profile, you need to think strategically about what you want to accomplish. Here are some tips for creating a quality profile:

- **Set goals for what you want to achieve on LinkedIn**—Are you looking for a job? Do you want to develop your business and find new clients? Are you a recruiter seeking passive job candidates? Make sure that everything you include in your profile works toward achieving that goal.

- **Make a list of keywords that relate to your experience, education, certifications, profession, and industry**—Every industry has its buzzwords, and you need to include these if they're terms a recruiter or potential client would search for. For example, an IT professional might include keywords such as Java, Oracle, SAP, or AJAX. A project manager might select PMP, PMI, UML, SDLC, or Six Sigma. A public relations professional, on the other hand, could choose PRSA, APR, or social media.

- **Have your current resume handy for easier profile completion**—You can refer to it for any necessary dates or other data you might have forgotten.

- **Check for spelling and grammar errors**—Nothing detracts more from a good profile than typos.

- **Remember that most people just scan your profile**—You need to capture their attention quickly and not overwhelm them with unnecessary details that detract from your goals.

- **Keep it professional**—A few personal details, such as your interests, help humanize your profile, but too much emphasis on outside activities detracts from your professional goals.

- **Don't duplicate your resume**—Remember, though, that a profile isn't a resume and shouldn't include the level of detail a resume does. A profile is a strategic summary of your professional background designed to achieve specific goals.

It's Not All Good

PROTECT YOUR PRIVACY

Keep privacy issues in mind as you complete your profile. Enter only data that you're willing to share publicly. In addition to reviewing your profile content for privacy issues, also review any media files you plan to upload for private information. For example, if you're a job seeker, you might not want to upload a copy of your resume that includes your address and personal phone number. Alternatively, remove any private information before uploading.

View Your Profile

To view your profile, click the Profile link on the LinkedIn menu. Your profile is rather empty when you first sign up for LinkedIn, but by the time you finish this chapter you should have a complete profile ready to showcase your professional accomplishments.

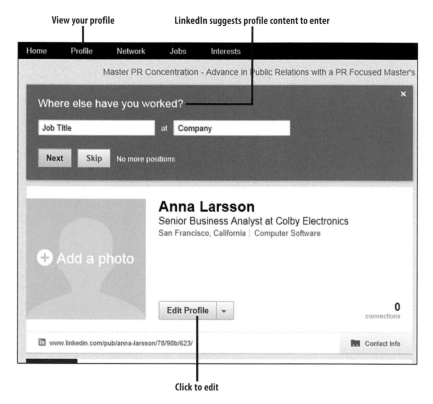

View your profile   LinkedIn suggests profile content to enter

Click to edit

>>>Go Further

UNDERSTANDING PROFILE STRENGTH

On the right side of your profile is the Profile Strength meter, which rates the effectiveness of your profile. When you first sign up for LinkedIn, you're rated a Beginner, but your profile strength increases as you add more profile content. The maximum profile strength is All-Star, which enables you to share your profile on Facebook and Twitter. Even more important, having an All-Star profiles encourages people to network with you and makes you far more likely to receive opportunities than people with incomplete profiles.

At a minimum, your profile should include the following items:

- Your current position
- At least two past positions
- Your education
- A profile summary
- A profile photo
- At least three recommendations

Just filling out basic profile fields, however, doesn't guarantee success. You also need the right profile content. A few words in a field might count toward a computer's view of "completeness," but it won't be effective if your profile still contains minimal information. In this chapter, you discover how to create a profile that LinkedIn rates as an All-Star and increases your chances of all-star results.

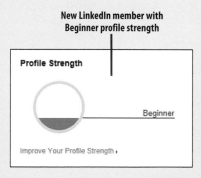

New LinkedIn member with Beginner profile strength

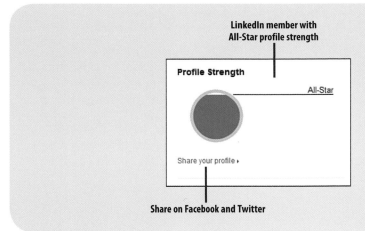

LinkedIn member with
All-Star profile strength

Profile Strength

All-Star

Share your profile ›

Share on Facebook and Twitter

Edit Your Profile

The Edit Profile page is where you perform most of the tasks in this chapter.

1. Select Edit Profile from the Profile menu.

2. Edit your profile content.

3. Click the Done Editing button (located at the top of your profile, next to your photo).

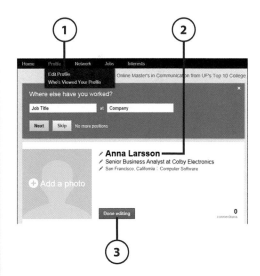

Entering Basic Profile Information

The Edit Profile page displays your name, title, company, location, and industry based on the data you entered when you signed up for LinkedIn. Even if this information is correct, you should review this section to determine whether you need to make any additional modifications.

For example, the name fields include some options not available when you sign up. In addition, you might want a more interesting headline than the default headline LinkedIn provides.

Edit Your Name

In addition to editing your name, you can add a former or maiden name or modify your display name.

1. Click the Edit icon next to your name.

2. Make any changes to your first and last name.

3. Click the Former Name link.

4. Optionally, enter your former name.

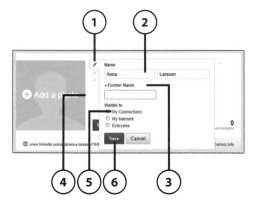

Displaying a Former or Maiden Name

If you've changed your name at any point during your career, it could be difficult for former classmates or colleagues to find you. Entering your former or maiden name makes it easier when people search for your former name.

5. Specify who can see your name: My Connections (1st degree connections only), My Network (people up to your 3rd degree connections), or Everyone.

6. Click the Save button.

Display Name Privacy

By default, LinkedIn displays your full name. If you have strong privacy concerns, you can choose to display only your first name and last initial to anyone other than your own connections.

Edit Your Headline

LinkedIn uses a combination of your title and company name as your professional headline, which should be sufficient for most people. You might want to customize this, however, if you're seeking work, are self-employed, or maintain more than one job. Some people include targeted keywords, professional certifications, or degrees in their professional headlines.

Some examples:

- PMP-certified IT Project Manager Seeking New Opportunities
- Bestselling Author | Weight Loss Coach | Certified Nutritionist
- Public Relations Executive, MBA, APR, Fellow PRSA

1. Click the Edit icon next to your headline.

2. Enter your new headline.

3. Click the Save button.

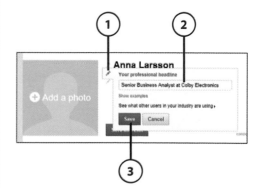

Edit Your Location and Industry

Entering your location and industry helps other LinkedIn members find you. If you don't want to enter your exact location (such as San Mateo, California), you can choose to display only a geographic area (such as San Francisco Bay Area).

1. Click the Edit icon next to your headline.

2. Select your country.

3. Enter your postal code.

4. Specify the location you want to display: your exact city or basic geographic area.

5. Select an industry that best reflects your professional experience.

6. Click the Save button.

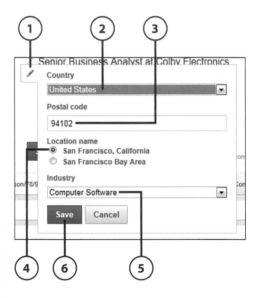

Add a Profile Photo

A photo helps bring your profile to life and sets you apart from other LinkedIn members. A professional headshot works best on your LinkedIn profile.

1. Click the Add a Photo link.

2. Click the Browse button to select a photo to upload. Depending on your browser or operating system, the name and features of the dialog box that opens could vary.

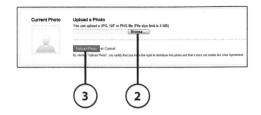

Photo Format and Size Limits

You can upload a photo in a JPG, GIF, or PNG file format. The file cannot be larger than 4MB.

3. Click the Upload Photo button.

4. Use LinkedIn's resizing tool to make any modifications.

5. Click the Save Photo button to complete the upload process.

6. Indicate your photo visibility preferences.

Photo Visibility

You can specify that your photo is visible to your connections, to your network, or to everyone. Note that your connections include only the people you directly connect with; your network includes the people connected to your connections.

7. Click the Save Settings button.

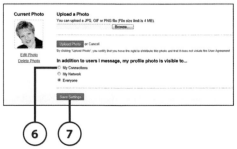

Easily Replace or Remove Your Photo

If you want to replace or remove your profile photo, click the Edit icon on your photo. You can upload a new photo or click the Delete Photo link to remove your photo.

Edit icon

Edit Your Contact Information

You can add optional contact information on the Edit Profile page, including your email address (by default, LinkedIn displays the address you used to sign up), phone, mailing address, or IM (instant message). This data displays to your connections, but not to anyone else on LinkedIn.

1. Click the Edit Contact Info link.

2. Click the Edit icon next to the field you want to edit.

3. Enter your data. In this example, you enter your phone number and select the type of phone (Mobile, Home, or Work).

4. Click the Save button.

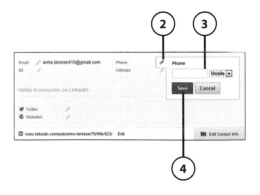

It's Not All Good

CONSIDER YOUR PERSONAL PRIVACY

Entering any data in the Contact Info section is optional. Carefully consider your personal privacy before making any personal information public, even to a restricted group of people.

Integrate Your LinkedIn Account with Twitter

If you have an account on Twitter (www.twitter.com), you might want to consider integrating it with LinkedIn. By doing so, you can share selected Twitter updates.

1. Click the Edit Contact Info link.

2. Click the Edit icon next to the Twitter field.

3. Click the Add Your Twitter account link.

4. Enter your Twitter username or email as well as your password. If you're already logged in to Twitter, LinkedIn skips this step.

5. Click the Authorize App button.

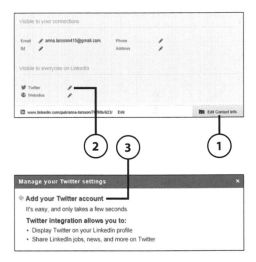

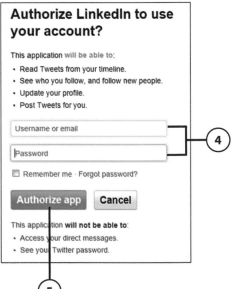

6. Click the Save Changes button.

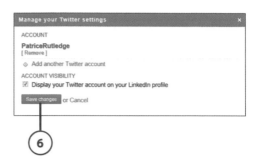

6

UNDERSTANDING HOW LINKEDIN INTEGRATES WITH TWITTER

When you add a Twitter account, LinkedIn does the following by default:

- Displays your Twitter username on your LinkedIn profile
- Shares tweets that contain the #in or #li hashtags on your LinkedIn status
- Displays a picture, page title, and short description with a link

If you want to change the default settings, remove a Twitter account, or add another Twitter account, click the Edit icon next to the Twitter field on the Edit Profile page. The Manage Your Twitter Settings dialog box opens, where you can manage how LinkedIn integrates with Twitter. Click the Save Changes button when you finish updating the settings in this dialog box.

You can also share your LinkedIn updates on Twitter by selecting the Twitter check box when you post updates (see Chapter 5, "Managing and Updating Your Profile").

Add Website Links

Listing your website, blog, portfolio, or other social site on LinkedIn
enables other members to find you
easily on the Web.

1. Click the Edit Contact Info link.

2. Click the Edit icon next to the
   Websites field.

3. From the Websites drop-down list,
   select the type of link you want to
   add.

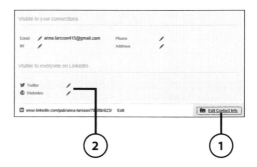

Gain Name Recognition for Your Sites

Options include Personal Website,
Company Website, Blog, RSS Feed,
Portfolio, and Other. If you select
Other, a text box appears in which
you can enter the name of your
choice. You can use the Other
option to gain name recognition
for your site or blog. For example,
if you have a blog called Project
Management Best Practices, you
might prefer to create a link with
that name rather than using the
generic "Website" or "Blog." In
addition, you can use this field to
link to your business's Facebook
page or other social sites.

4. Enter the complete URL of the site
   you want to link to, such as http://
   www.patricerutledge.com.

5. Click the Save button.

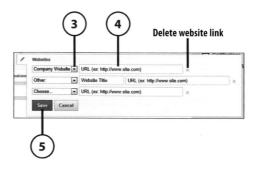

Delete website link

You Can List a Maximum of Three Sites

To avoid clutter and prevent link spam, you can enter only three websites on your LinkedIn profile. If you have more than three sites to consider, think carefully about which sites would generate the most interest on a business networking site such as LinkedIn.

Add a Profile Summary

The Background section on the Edit Profile page asks you to enter a profile summary. This is an important step because people scanning your profile often read this section first.

Review Other Profiles in Your Industry

To get some ideas about what to include in your summary section, analyze the profiles of others in your profession or industry. Each industry has its own buzzwords and "personality," so what works for one professional might not be as appropriate for another.

1.   Click the Add a Summary link.

Consider Adding Media Files

You can also add media files to your summary, such as documents you upload or links to content on SlideShare, YouTube, or other sites. See "Adding Media Files," later in this chapter.

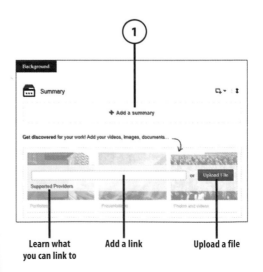

Learn what you can link to

Add a link

Upload a file

2. Enter a summary of your professional experience and goals.

Summary Tips

In addition to summarizing your professional experience, you can also use this field to indicate that you're looking for job opportunities (assuming you're currently unemployed), recruiting staff, accepting new clients, or seeking new business partners, for example. Be sure to keep it professional, however. This is not the place for an advertisement or sales hype.

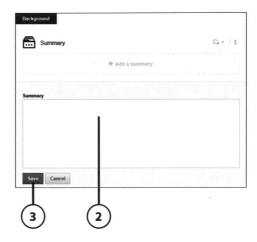

3. Click the Save button.

Edit Your Current Position

Although you already entered your current job title and company when you created your LinkedIn account, you need to expand on that basic information.

1. Click the Edit link next to your current position.

Add another position

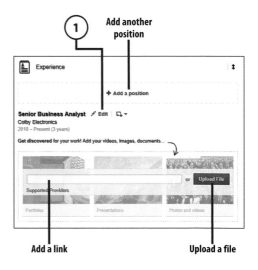

Add a link

Upload a file

2. Optionally, click the Change Company link to change the company name you initially entered.

3. Enter the location of this company.

4. Select the period of your employment from the drop-down lists.

5. Select the I Currently Work Here check box if this is your current position.

6. Enter a brief description of your current position.

7. Click the Save button.

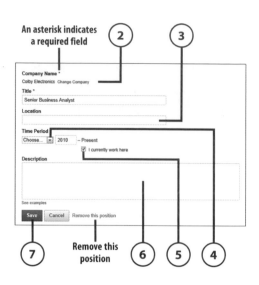

An asterisk indicates a required field

Remove this position

PICKING THE RIGHT COMPANY NAME

>>>Go Further

If your company has a LinkedIn Company Page, you can display your company logo and include a link to this page from your profile. This also makes it easier for your colleagues to find you. To do so, you need to select the right Company Page from the drop-down list that displays when you click the Change Company link. In most cases, it should be easy to find your company in the list. If you work for a large corporation with many divisions, each having its own Company Page, you need to be sure to select the right one. If you have any doubts, check the profiles of your colleagues to verify which Company Page they're linking to.

CREATING A QUALITY DESCRIPTION

Here are a few tips on what to include in the Description field:

- **Use keywords**—Think of the terms people would search for and use them in your description. For example, if you work in IT, mention actual technologies rather than vague generalizations.

- **Emphasize accomplishments over job duties**—For example, rather than saying that you're responsible for sales, focus on your sales achievements and awards.

- **Be brief**—The Description field is a summary, not a detailed resume.

- **Keep your goals in mind**—If you want to attract recruiters, think about what would interest them in a potential candidate. If you're seeking clients for your business, focus on what would make them want to hire you.

Add a Previous Position

In addition to listing your current position, you should add previous positions on the Edit Profile page. Adding past positions is important because it provides a clearer view of your background and makes it easier to connect with your former colleagues at previous companies.

Deciding How Many Positions to Add

If you have limited work experience, list all your previous positions. If you have extensive experience, it's a good idea to focus only on the past 10 to 15 years of your work life unless an early position in your career is very relevant to your current goals.

1. Click the Add a Position link.

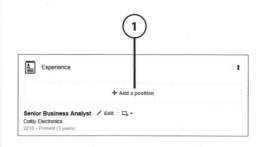

2. Enter the details about this position. See "Edit Your Current Position," earlier in this chapter, for more information about entering position data.

3. Click the Save button.

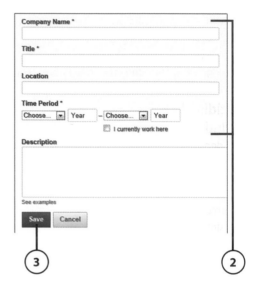

Add Educational Information

Next, you add information about your educational background. LinkedIn also uses this information to help you connect easily with former classmates.

1. Click the Add Education link.

2. Start typing the name of your school in the School Name field and then select it from the drop-down list that displays. If you can't find your school in the list, you can enter it manually.

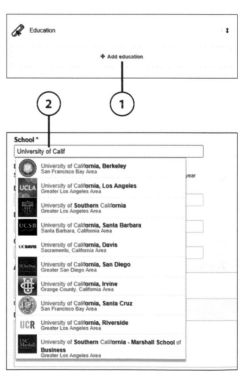

3. Optionally, in the Dates Attended fields, enter the years you attended. If you're still a student, enter your anticipated year of graduation in the second field.

Deciding Whether to Include Graduation Years

The decision whether to include your year of graduation is a personal choice for many experienced professionals. LinkedIn doesn't require you to list the year you graduated; this is an optional field. Keep in mind, however, that LinkedIn won't be able to automatically search for your former classmates if you omit your graduation year. You would need to perform a manual search for former classmates.

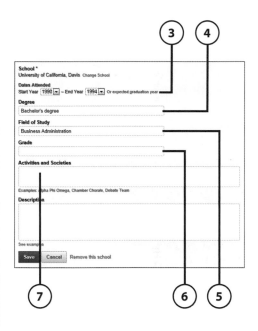

4. Enter your degree from the drop-down list, such as Bachelor of Arts (BA).

5. Enter your field of study. This can be your major, an area of concentration, or the name of a certificate.

6. Enter your GPA (grade point average) in the Grade field. This is more meaningful to recent graduates than to experienced professionals.

7. List relevant activities in the Activities and Societies field. This might include honors, study abroad, and any extracurricular activities.

Enter Only Relevant Information

You don't need to complete all the fields in the Education section to provide an accurate picture of your educational background. For example, details about your participation with the ski club or theater group 20 years ago won't add real value to your LinkedIn profile unless they relate to your current career. Entering the most pertinent data ensures that people who read your profile focus on what's relevant.

8. Enter a description of your educational experience.

9. Click the Save button.

EDUCATION SECTION BEST PRACTICES

Consider the following best practices when choosing which educational information to enter:

- Include colleges and universities from which you received a degree.

- Include *relevant* certificates and continuing education coursework. For example, if you're looking for a job in a new field and have completed a related certificate, you should include this information.

- Don't include every continuing education course or seminar you've ever taken. It's important to be strategic, not prolific.

- Don't include your high school information unless you're still in college, are a recent graduate, or specifically want to reconnect with high school classmates.

Add Your Interests

Optionally, you can add a list of personal interests to your profile.

Interests Versus Skills

Interests refer to personal interests such as sailing, yoga, wine tasting, triathlons, green building, 19th century antiques, or any other topics that help your profile readers get a better idea of who you are as a person. *Skills* refer to specific job qualifications such as copywriting, marketing, executive management, Photoshop, Java, and so forth. You should enter your professional interests or skills in the Skills & Expertise profile section, described in the "Add Your Skills and Expertise" section later in this chapter.

1. Click the Edit link next to the Interests field.

2. Enter your interests in the text box.

3. Click the Save button.

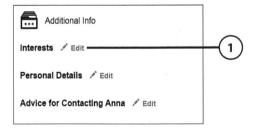

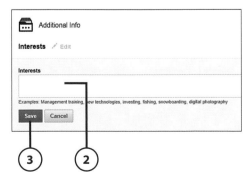

Add Personal Details

Another profile option is to add personal details, such as your birthday or marital status. If you choose to enter this data, LinkedIn enables you to control who can view your entries. LinkedIn also notifies your connections when it's your birthday, which can be a good way to stay in touch with your network. For example, if you choose to make your birthday visible to your connections, LinkedIn could send them an email notification and display a birthday announcement on their home pages (depending on the account settings they select).

Protecting Your Privacy

If you do choose to share either your birthday or your marital status online, consider carefully the visibility settings you select. My personal preference is to share my birth month and day only with my 1st degree connections (to take advantage of LinkedIn's birthday promotions) and not to enter my birthday year or marital status.

1. Click the Edit link next to the Personal Details field.

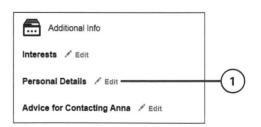

2. Select your information as appropriate for Birthday Month, Day, and Year from the drop-down lists.

3. Select your marital status from the drop-down list.

4. Click the Lock icon to manage visibility settings for each active field.

5. Specify who can see this data: Only Me, My Connections (1st degree connections only), My Network (people up to 3rd degrees away from you), or Everyone.

6. Click the Close button.

7. Repeat steps 4 through 6 for all other fields for which you selected data.

8. Click the Save button.

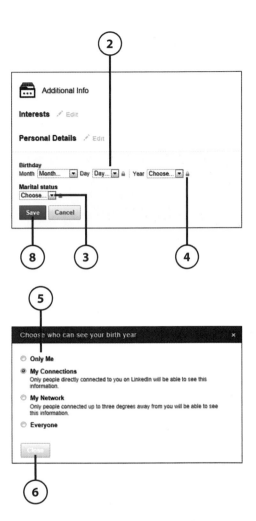

Enter Contact Details

A third option in the Additional Info section enables you to give advice to people who want to contact you. The information you enter here is public and visible to anyone who views your profile.

Contact Details Tips

For example, if one of your LinkedIn goals is to generate business leads or drive traffic to your website, you could enter your website URL or phone number with encouragement to contact you (no sales pitches, though). Alternatively, you could use this section to indicate that you're open to networking with new people in your field, prefer connecting only with people you know, and so forth.

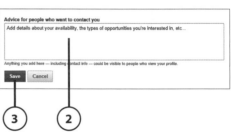

1. Click the Edit link next to the Advice for Contacting [Your First Name] field.

2. Enter your advice in the text box.

3. Click the Save button.

Add Your Skills and Expertise

LinkedIn enables you to add up to 50 skills on your profile. In addition to showcasing your talents and expertise, the Skills & Expertise section lets your connections endorse you for these skills in a single click.

See Chapter 12, "Working with LinkedIn Endorsements," for more information on managing your skills and getting endorsements for them.

Skills & Expertise section with numerous endorsements

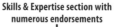

1. Click the Add Skills & Expertise link.

2. Start typing the skill you want to add. LinkedIn displays a list of potential matches you can choose.

3. Click the Add button.

4. Continue adding additional skills.

5. Click the Save button when you're finished.

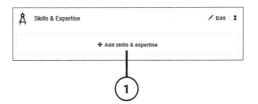

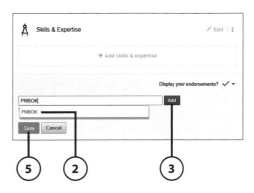

Finding Skills to List

If you're not sure which skills to list, review the profiles of your colleagues or others in your industry for inspiration.

Adding Media Files

On the Edit Profile page, you can enhance your profile by adding multimedia work samples such as images, videos, audio files, PDF documents, presentations, portfolios, and more. LinkedIn offers two options: upload a file from your computer, and insert a link to a file on a supported website such as SlideShare, Behance, or YouTube. Linking to a website or a favorite blog post is another option. You can add media files to the Summary, Education, or Experience sections.

People who visit your profile can click a media file to open it in a viewer where they can see it in more detail, like it, or add a comment.

Link to a website   SlideShare presentation   YouTube video

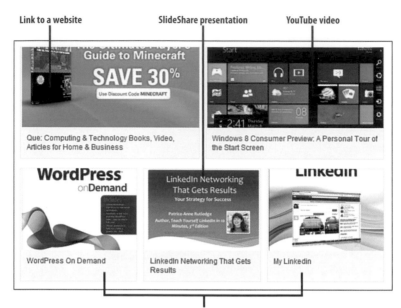

Uploaded images from your computer

View original   Media viewer   Like this content

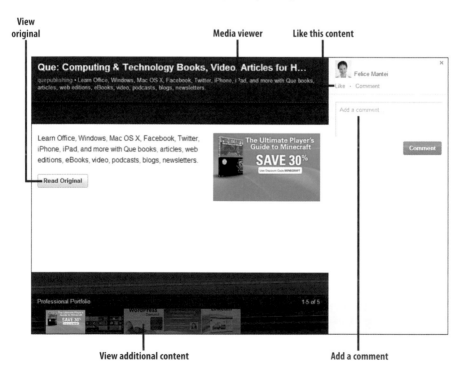

View additional content   Add a comment

Plan Before Posting

It's important to have a plan before adding media files to your profile. Although incorporating multimedia content can help your profile stand out from the crowd, ensure the files you add complement your LinkedIn business goals. Posting a few selected files with a distinct purpose is better than overwhelming your profile visitors with dozens of files.

Upload a File

1. Click the Media icon in the section where you want to upload your file and select Upload File from the drop-down menu.

Another way to upload a file

Alternate Method for Uploading Files

You can also click the Upload File button in the media box to upload a file.

2. Select the file you want to upload.

3. Click the Open button. Depending on your operating system or browser, this button could have another name.

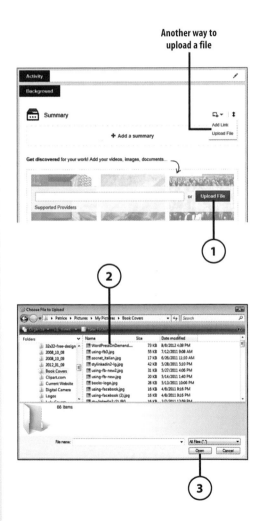

4. LinkedIn displays the file you uploaded.

5. Enter a title. By default, LinkedIn uses the file name, but you can edit this.

6. Enter an optional description.

7. Click the Save button.

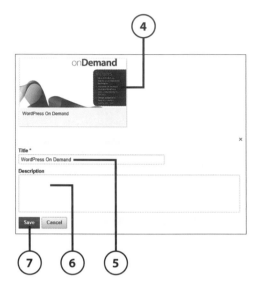

SUPPORTED FILE FORMATS FOR UPLOADS

You can upload files no larger than 100MB in the following formats:

Presentations	Documents	Images
.pdf	.pdf	.png
.ppt	.doc	.gif
.pps	.docx	.jpg
.pptx	.rtf	.jpeg
.ppsx	.odt	
.pot		
.potx		
.odp		

Link to a URL

1. Click the Media icon in the section where you want to link to your file and select Add Link from the drop-down menu.

Alternative Method for Linking to Files

You can also enter your URL in the media box and press the Enter key.

2. Enter the URL of the site you want to link to.

3. LinkedIn displays the file or website you linked to.

Can I Change the Featured Image?

LinkedIn selects a featured image to display for each media file. You can't change this image.

4. Enter a title. By default, LinkedIn uses the filename, but you can edit this.

5. Enter an optional description.

6. Click the Save button.

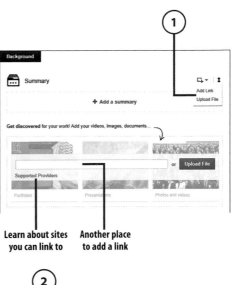

Learn about sites   **Another place**
you can link to   **to add a link**

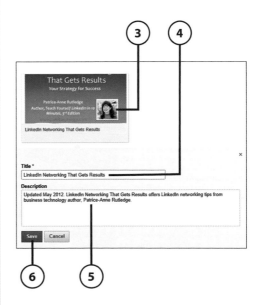

>>>Go Further

SUPPORTED CONTENT PROVIDERS

LinkedIn supports a long list of content providers (sites you can link to), including many popular image, audio, video, and presentation sites. Here's a brief list of the most popular content providers.

Image	Audio	Video	Presentation and Other Providers
ow.ly	AudioBoo	ABC News	Prezi
pikchur	SoundCloud	Animoto	Scribd
twitgoo	Spotify	blip	SlideShare
twitpic		brightcove	Behance
TwitrPix		CBS News	Issuu
Twitter		CNBC	Kickstarter
		CNN	Quantcast
		Forbes	
		Hulu	
		Vimeo	
		YouTube	

To view a complete list of current content providers, click the Supported Providers link on the Edit Profile page.

Edit a Media File

1. Click the Edit icon on a media file.

2. Edit the data about this file.

3. Click the Save button.

Move a Media File

1. Click the Edit icon on a media file.

2. Select a new location for this file from the Move This Media To drop-down list. Your options include moving to your LinkedIn summary or a listed position or educational institution.

3. Click the Save button.

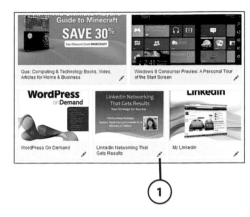

Rearranging Media Files

In addition to moving media files to another profile section, you can rearrange media files in the same section by dragging and dropping them to a new position.

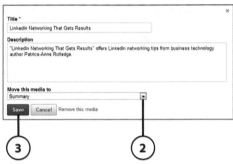

Remove a Media File

1. Click the Edit icon on a media file.

2. Click the Remove This Media link.

3. Click the Yes, Remove It button to confirm removal.

Adding Profile Sections

LinkedIn enables you to enhance your profile with optional sections that highlight additional professional accomplishments. You can add the following optional profile sections:

- Projects
- Languages
- Publications
- Organizations
- Honors & Awards

- Test Scores
- Courses
- Patents
- Certifications
- Volunteering & Causes

It's Not All Good

DON'T OVERDO IT WITH ADDITIONAL SECTIONS

Sections should add value to your profile, not fill it with irrelevant information. Remember that you don't need to add every optional section to your profile—and probably shouldn't. Instead, focus on adding only content that aligns with your LinkedIn goals and enhances your professional reputation. For example, listing courses and test scores is great for students and recent graduates, but it's less important for those with significant experience who graduated years ago.

Although adding appropriate sections is definitely worthwhile, having too much information on your profile is almost as bad as having a profile with scant details. Most people don't want to spend too much time viewing a profile, and if yours is filled with extensive irrelevant information, they might move on to the next person before discovering what you can really offer.

Add a Section

In this example, you add a project to your profile. Adding other sections follows similar steps.

1. Click Projects on the right column of your profile.

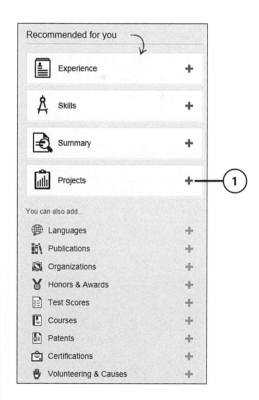

2. Enter a project name.

3. Select the occupation related to this project. You can choose any of the positions on your profile from the drop-down list.

4. Select the date this project occurred.

5. Enter a project URL if this project has a website.

6. Start typing the name of any additional team members in the Add Team Member field, and select a match from the drop-down list. (Only your 1st degree connections are available.)

7. Repeat step 7 to add more team members if necessary.

8. Enter a project description.

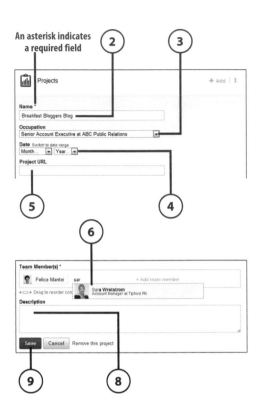

Description Tips

If you include other team members on your project and want them to display this project on their profile, be sure to write an objective third-person description and not a first-person description. You want the description to apply to all team members, not just you and your role in the project.

9. Click Save.

What Happens Next?

LinkedIn displays your project on your profile and notifies additional team members about the project. They can choose whether to display the project on their profile.

Group project displayed on profile

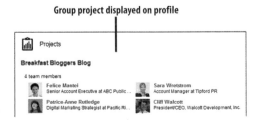

REARRANGING PROFILE CONTENT

Optionally, you can rearrange the sections on your profile. This is useful if you want to highlight your most important achievements at the top of your profile rather than keep LinkedIn's default section order. Click the Reorder Section icon and drag it to your preferred profile location.

Drag to move this section

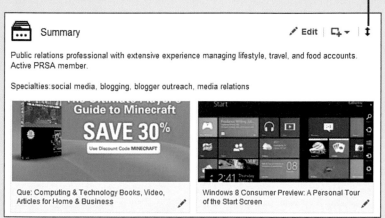

REVIEWING YOUR PROFILE

Before sharing your profile with the world, be sure to review it carefully. Click the Profile link on the LinkedIn main menu to view your profile as other LinkedIn members would see it. Check for content accuracy as well as for grammar and spelling errors. If necessary, return to the Edit Profile page to revise any of your entries.

Customizing Your Public Profile and URL

LinkedIn makes a public version of your profile available to all web users, regardless of whether they're LinkedIn members or connected to you. When someone searches your name on Google or Yahoo!, for example, the public version of your profile appears in search results. Although a public profile is a great way to promote your career and gain visibility, it isn't for everyone. Don't worry. You have control over exactly what others can view on your profile. You can even hide your profile from public view if you choose.

Your LinkedIn profile appears in Google search results

Customize Your Public Profile

You can specify exactly which fields are visible on your public profile in the Customize Your Public Profile box.

1. Click the Edit link to the right of your public profile URL.

2. The Customize Your Public Profile box displays on the right side of the Edit Profile page.

3. Select the check box next to any unselected field you want to display.

4. Deselect the check box next to any selected field you don't want to display.

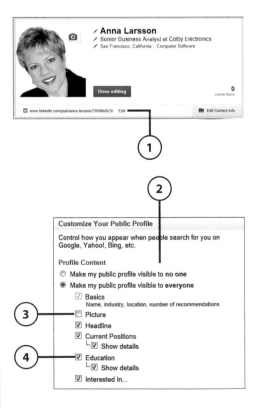

Hide Your Public Profile

By default, your public profile is visible to everyone. Optionally, you can hide it if you don't want people to find your LinkedIn profile on the Web.

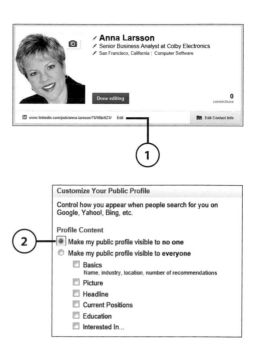

1. Click the Edit link to the right of your public profile URL.

2. Select the Make My Public Profile Visible to No One option button in the Customize Your Public Profile box.

Customize Your Public Profile URL

By default, your public LinkedIn URL looks something like this: http://www.linkedin.com/pub/patrice-rutledge/13/521/845. The numbers in this URL address aren't very user-friendly, however, so customize your public profile URL to something easier to remember, such as www.linkedin.com/in/patriceannerutledge.

1. Click the Edit link to the right of your Public Profile URL.

2. The Your Public Profile URL box displays on the right side of the Edit Profile page.

3. Click the Customize Your Public Profile URL link.

4. Enter the custom URL you prefer
   in the Customize Your Public
   Profile dialog box.

Naming Suggestions

Using your first name and last
name as one string of characters
is a good choice. Spaces, symbols,
and special characters aren't
allowed in your URL. If someone
else is already using the URL you
want, LinkedIn lets you know and
offers several available alterna-
tives based on your first and last
name.

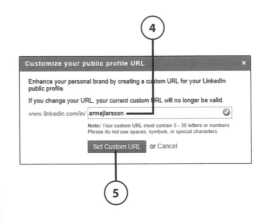

5. Click the Set Custom URL button.

Create a Profile Badge

To promote your LinkedIn on your
website or blog, you can add a
badge. For example, a blog sidebar is
a great place for a LinkedIn button.

1. Click the Edit link to the right of
   your Public Profile URL.

2. Click the Create a Profile Badge
   link in the Your Public Profile URL
   box.

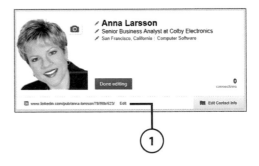

3. Copy the code next to the badge style you want to display.

4. Paste the code on your own site.

What Do I Do with This Code?

The exact steps for inserting this code into your website vary based on the tool you use to create your site. Many website tools provide an automated way to include social buttons on your site that enable you to simply enter your LinkedIn URL rather than insert code.

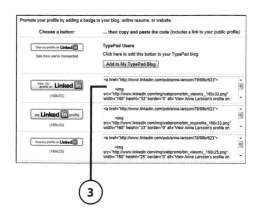

Exploring Other Profile Options

After creating your profile, take a minute to explore the profile options available when you click the down arrow next to the Edit Profile link on the Your Profile page (click Profile on the LinkedIn menu to access). The options on this menu include

- **Ask to Be Recommended**—Send a recommendation request to one of your connections. See Chapter 11, "Working with LinkedIn Recommendations," for more information.

- **Create Profile in Another Language**—This is mostly useful if you speak another language fluently and want to attract clients or potential employers who speak this language.

- **Share Profile**—Share your profile on Facebook or Twitter.

- **Export to PDF**—Keep an offline copy of your profile by exporting to a PDF.

- **Manage Public Profile Settings**—Manage the settings you explored in the "Customizing Your Public Profile URL" section in this chapter.

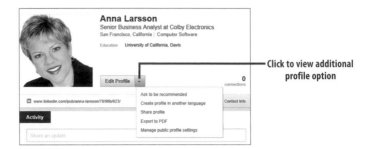

Click to view additional profile option

Manage your LinkedIn connections on the Contacts page

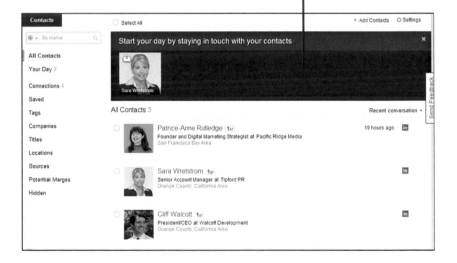

In this chapter, you explore how to develop a solid LinkedIn connection strategy, connect with other members, and manage your contacts.

→ Developing a connection strategy
→ Importing email contacts
→ Finding and connecting with alumni
→ Sending and responding to invitations
→ Managing your connections

Developing Your LinkedIn Network

After creating a strong profile, the next step in making the most of your LinkedIn experience is developing a solid network of professional connections. Before you add connections to LinkedIn, however, you should develop a connection strategy that matches your goals and networking philosophy.

Developing a Connection Strategy

There is no one "right" way to develop your LinkedIn network. All LinkedIn members are unique and need to follow a personalized strategy that focuses on their own goals, industry, position, and comfort level with networking.

The three most common approaches are as follows:

- **Connect only with people you know**—LinkedIn members who follow this approach connect only with colleagues, classmates, and associates they personally know or who their known connections recommend to them.

- **Connect with people you know plus strategic contacts you would like to know**—With this approach, you connect with people you know and seek out strategic connections who match your networking goals.

- **Connect with anyone and everyone**—Some LinkedIn members, particularly those who want to use the site for business development purposes, are open networkers and like to connect with as many people as possible and make special efforts to connect with thousands of people.

What's an Open Networker?

As you begin to use LinkedIn, you might see the terms *open networker* or *LION* on member profiles. An open networker is a LinkedIn member who is open to connecting with people they don't know. Several LinkedIn groups exist for open networkers, such as LION (LinkedIn Open Networker) and TopLinked. Although it's a good idea to network with new people and develop a mutually beneficial business relationship, be careful not to abuse open networking by connecting indiscriminately just to amass a large network. Don't treat your LinkedIn network as a numbers game.

Which approach is best? There is no one right answer for everyone. All LinkedIn members have their own goals for what they hope to accomplish on the site as well as their own networking strategies and comfort levels.

To get started, consider connecting with current and former colleagues, current and former classmates, friends, and fellow members of professional associations. Then expand your network from there based on your personal goals and preferences.

Building Your Network

LinkedIn offers several ways to build your network. You can

- Import your webmail or desktop email contacts and search for them on LinkedIn. The Import Contacts and Invite page enables you to import contacts from Gmail, Outlook, Yahoo! Mail, Hotmail, AOL, and other email providers. See the section "Import Your Gmail Contacts," for one example of the contact-import process. When you're new to LinkedIn, your home page also prompts you to import your contacts.

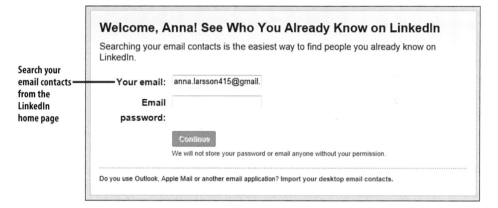

Search your email contacts from the LinkedIn home page

- View the People You May Know box on your home page for potential connections.

LinkedIn analyzes your network for people you might know

- Search for and connect with alumni on the Alumni page. See the section "Find and Connect with Alumni," later in this chapter.

- Search for and connect with people you know using LinkedIn's advanced search functionality. See Chapter 7, "Searching on LinkedIn," for more information.

- Send an invitation request to someone who doesn't use LinkedIn yet. See the section "Connect with People Not on LinkedIn," later in this chapter.

Keep in mind that you don't need to use all these methods to develop your pool of LinkedIn connections. For example, you might not want to connect with all your webmail or address book contacts. Or your webmail account might contain personal email addresses, not the email addresses your contacts used to sign up for LinkedIn.

Import Email Contacts

The Import Contacts and Invite page enables you to import your contacts from popular email providers such as Gmail, Outlook, Yahoo! Mail, Hotmail/Outlook.com, and AOL. To access this page, select Add Connections from the Network menu.

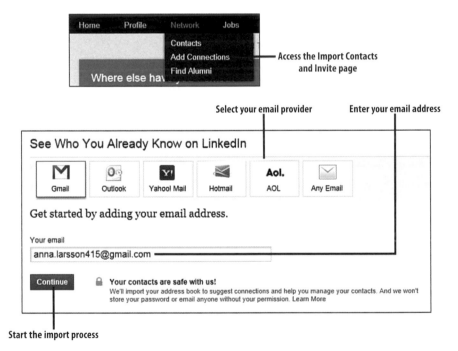

The exact steps for importing vary based on your email provider, but the process involves connecting with your provider and displaying a list of email contacts who are LinkedIn members. From here, you can select the people you want to invite to connect on LinkedIn.

If your email provider doesn't appear on the Import Contacts and Invite page, click the Any Email button. You can import from other providers including Comcast, Cox, AT&T, Verizon, EarthLink, MSN, and more.

Click for more options

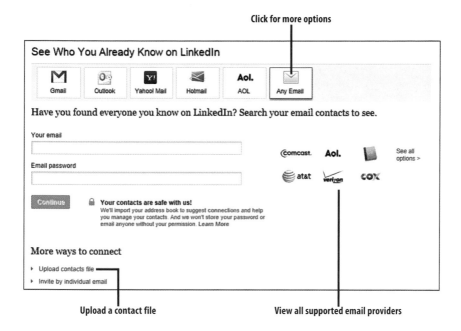

Upload a contact file   View all supported email providers

Import Your Gmail Contacts

In this example, you import Gmail contacts. Even if you use one of the many other email providers LinkedIn supports, this should give you a good idea of the process involved.

1. Select Add Connections from the Network menu.

2. Select the Gmail button.

3. Enter your Gmail email address.

4. Click the Continue button.

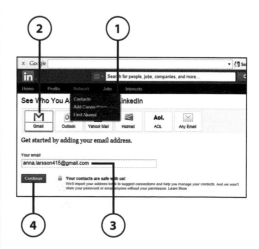

5. LinkedIn connects with your Gmail account and displays a list of contacts who are LinkedIn members.

6. By default, LinkedIn selects the check box next to each person on the list. Deselect the check box next to the names of the people you don't want to connect with.

7. Click the Add Connection(s) button.

8. LinkedIn sends invitations to the selected people.

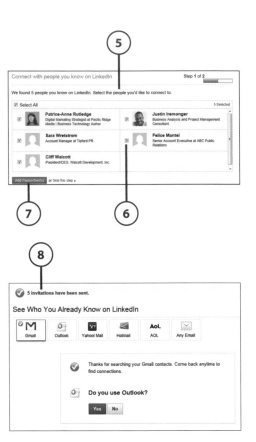

What Happens Next?

Each selected person receives an individual invitation from LinkedIn and must manually accept it to become one of your connections. (See the section "Respond to an Invitation," later in this chapter for more information.)

If you have another email account whose contacts you want to import, you can repeat this process. For example, you might have a work email address and a personal email address, each with different contacts.

Find and Connect with Alumni

LinkedIn enables you to quickly identify former classmates you might want to connect with.

1. Select Find Alumni from the Network menu.

2. LinkedIn displays a list of alumni from the most recent school listed on your profile.

3. Click the Connect button below a person's name to send an invitation to this person.

Narrowing Your Results

If you attended a large school, you could discover a lengthy list of potential classmates. Optionally, you can narrow your results by attendance date, location, employer, or occupation. You can also search the Alumni page by name or keyword.

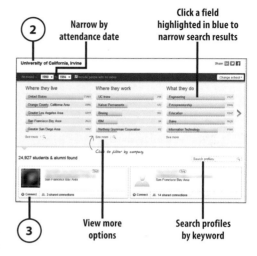

Narrow by attendance date

Click a field highlighted in blue to narrow search results

View more options

Search profiles by keyword

Send an Invitation to Connect

The exact process of connecting on LinkedIn varies based on where you initiate the invitation, but, in general, you click either the Connect button or the Connect link to send an invitation. In this example, you send an invitation to someone who displays in the People You May Know box on the LinkedIn home page.

Sending Invitations to People You Don't Know

If you don't know someone and don't have any connection with this person (such as a common profession, association membership, or alumni affiliation), be sure to make your reason for wanting to connect clear so that the recipient doesn't mark your request as spam. Optionally, consider sending an InMail or requesting an introduction instead. See Chapter 6, "Communicating with Other LinkedIn Members," for more information on InMail and introductions.

1. Click the Connect link below the person to whom you want to send an invitation.

2. Specify how you know this person.

3. Include a personal note in the text box explaining why you want to connect on LinkedIn. This is particularly important if you don't know the person you want to connect with.

4. Click the Send Invitation button.

What Happens Next?

LinkedIn sends this person your invitation, who must accept it manually to become one of your connections. (See the section "Respond to an Invitation," later in this chapter for more information about this process).

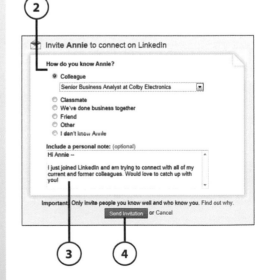

UNDERSTANDING INVITATION OPTIONS

Depending on which option you select when sending an invitation, LinkedIn might prompt you for additional information.

- **Colleague**—Select a company from the drop-down list that appears.

- **Classmate**—Select a school from the drop-down list that appears.

- **We've Done Business Together**—Select a company from the drop-down list that appears.

- **Friend**—LinkedIn requires no additional information.

- **Groups**—Select a LinkedIn group from the drop-down list that appears. This option doesn't display if you don't share a common group with this person.

- **Other**—Enter the person's email address.

- **I Don't Know [First Name]**—LinkedIn requires no additional information.

Connect with People Not on LinkedIn

If you discover that some of your real-world contacts aren't using LinkedIn yet, it's easy to invite them.

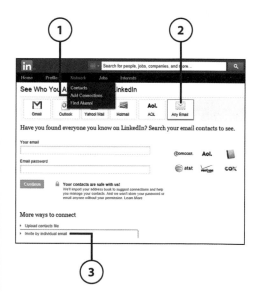

1. Select Add Connections from the Network menu.

2. Click the Any Email button.

3. Click the Invite by Individual Email link.

4. Enter the email address of the person or persons you want to invite. Separate multiple addresses with a comma.

5. Click the Send Invitations button.

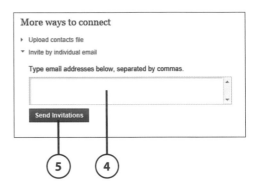

Respond to an Invitation

In addition to sending invitations to connect, you might receive invitations. LinkedIn makes it easy to accept—or ignore—invitations right from the navigation bar.

1. Pause over the Inbox button on the navigation bar.

2. LinkedIn displays a list of your most recent invitations and messages.

3. Pause over an invitation and click the Accept button to make this person a connection.

4. Pause over an invitation and click the Ignore button to ignore this request.

5. Click the sender's name if you would like to view the profile of a person who wants to connect.

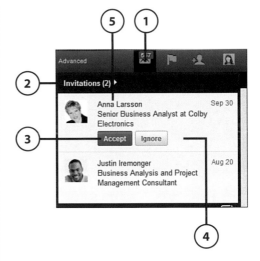

Ignoring an Invitation

When you ignore an invitation, LinkedIn moves it to your Archived folder where you can view and respond later. After ignoring an invitation, LinkedIn provides two additional options: the I Don't Know [First Name] link and the Report as Spam link. Clicking the I Don't Know link blocks this person from inviting you again and alerts LinkedIn that this was an unwanted invitation request. Clicking the Report as Spam link reports the sender to LinkedIn.

It's Not All Good

THINK CAREFULLY BEFORE REPORTING AN INVITATION

Because LinkedIn can penalize other members for sending too many requests to people they don't know—or for sending spam—think carefully before choosing these options. Selecting one of these options is too harsh if it's a genuine request from someone you just don't want to connect with.

Previewing a Profile

Previewing a LinkedIn member's profile can help you remember more about someone you don't know well or decide whether to connect with someone you don't know at all. If you do decide to connect, you can click the Accept Invitation button on the profile. This button displays only on profiles of people who have a pending invitation request.

Anna Larsson
Senior Business Analyst at Colby Electronics
San Francisco, California | Computer Software

Education   University of California, Davis

Accept Invitation   Contact Anna

Contact Info   www.linkedin.com/pub/anna-larsson/78/98b/623/

Click the Accept Invitation button on a profile

What Happens Next?

When you accept an invitation, LinkedIn makes this person a 1st degree connection in your network, whose updates display on your home page. You can also exchange messages with this connection.

OTHER WAYS TO REVIEW INVITATIONS

>>>Go Further

Although the easiest way to review invitations is from the navigation bar, LinkedIn offers two additional options. You can also

- Review, accept, and ignore invitations in your inbox. See Chapter 6 for more information about working with your inbox.

- Receive invitations to connect by email, if you specified that you want to receive email invitations on the Account & Settings page. (See Chapter 4, "Customizing Your LinkedIn Settings," for details.) Click the link in the email to open the invitation.

Review invitations in your inbox

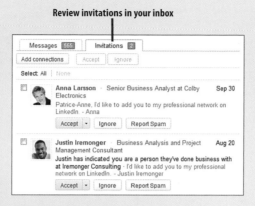

EXPANDING YOUR NETWORK

By now, you should have a good start on developing your LinkedIn network. Here are a few other suggestions for finding other worthwhile connections on LinkedIn:

- **Review the list of people your connections are connected to, which displays on their profile**—It's likely that you know some of the same people and would like to connect with them as well.

- **Search for individuals by name in the Search box at the top of LinkedIn**—LinkedIn displays a drop-down list where you can select the appropriate person.

- **Search by keyword and location to find local members of your professional associations**—For example, you could search for the keyword PRSA (for the Public Relations Society of America) and the postal code 92606 within a 25-mile radius to find fellow PRSA members in Orange County, California.

- **Search for potential connections among the members of any LinkedIn groups to which you belong**—Remember, however, not to spam fellow group members with connection invitations. Be selective in determining who you want to connect with.

See Chapter 7 for more information on searching for people.

>>>Go Further

Managing Your Connections

After you develop your LinkedIn network, you need an easy way to find and manage your connections. The Contacts page offers several ways to do this. Select Contacts from the Network menu to open this page, which displays previews of your connections and saved profiles.

Search by keyword | View connections with birthdays or new jobs | Synchronize with external sources

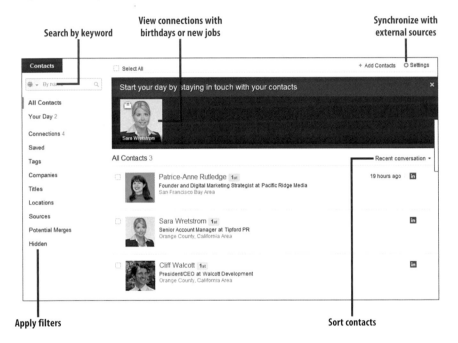

Apply filters | Sort contacts

The Contacts page offers a variety of options for managing your LinkedIn network, including the following:

- View connections with recent milestones such as a new job or birthday.

- Sort by recent conversations (the default), newly added, alphabetical, company, location, or those with whom you've lost touch.

- Search for people by keyword.

- Filter by specific criteria such as company, title, or location. This is particularly useful if you have a large network.

- View profiles you saved by clicking the Saved link.

Saving Profiles

The Saved tab displays the profiles of LinkedIn members you saved, even if they're not your connections. Saving profiles is an excellent way to track prospects, such as potential employers or clients. See Chapter 7 for more information on saving profiles.

- Hover over a preview to tag, message, hide, or remove this person.

Hover over a contact for more options

- Click a name to open this person's profile.

- Synchronize your LinkedIn contact with external sources.

Synchronizing Your Contact

Optionally, click the Settings link to synchronize your LinkedIn contacts with your contacts on sources including Microsoft Outlook, Google Gmail, Google Calendar, Google Contacts, Google Voice, Evernote, LinkedIn CardMunch, and many others. You can also manually import your contacts from an Outlook Contacts file, a Mac Address Book vCard file, or a Yahoo! Contacts file.

Add a Tag

Tags enable you to categorize your LinkedIn network using custom labels. By default, LinkedIn offers a "Favorites" tag, but you can create and use any tags you like. For example, you might want to tag people who belong to a common professional organization, prospective clients, and so forth. You can tag the profiles of your 1st degree connections as well as profiles you've saved.

1. Select Contacts from the Network menu.

2. Hover over the profile of the person you want to tag and click the Tag link.

3. Select the check box next to the tag or tags you want to apply.

4. Optionally, click the Add New Tags link to add a new tag.

Managing Your Tags

Click the Manage Tags link to open the Manage Tags dialog box. Here, you can edit or delete the tags you created.

Manage your tags

5. Enter a new tag in the text box and click the Save button.

6. Repeat steps 4 and 5 to add more tags.

7. LinkedIn displays the tags you applied below the photo of the tagged person.

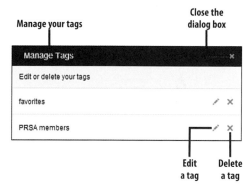

Manage your tags

Close the dialog box

Edit a tag   Delete a tag

Remove a Connection

If you decide that you no longer want to connect with someone on LinkedIn, you can remove that person as a connection. People you remove are no longer able to view any data restricted to actual connections, and they can't send you direct messages. LinkedIn, however, doesn't notify them that they've been removed.

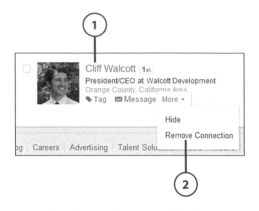

1. On the Contacts page, hover over the profile of the connection you want to remove.

2. Select Remove Connection from the More drop-down list.

3. Click the Remove button to confirm removal.

It's Not All Good

REMOVE CONNECTIONS FOR THE RIGHT REASON

Be sure that a connection really warrants removal before proceeding with the removal process. For example, if a connection you don't know well is bothering you with requests, spam, or sales pitches, this person is probably a connection worth removing. Removing former colleagues or associates simply because you haven't seen them in a while or don't work with them anymore can be shortsighted.

Editing Contact Info on a Profile

When you connect with another LinkedIn member or save someone's profile, LinkedIn activates the Relationship and Contact Info tabs on this person's profile.

The Relationship tab enables you to add and view notes, reminders, tags, and details about how you met this person. Some of this information displays automatically based on your interaction on LinkedIn; other data you must enter manually.

Add notes or reminders

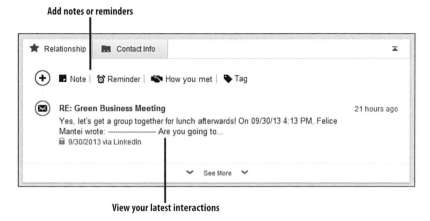

View your latest interactions

The Contact Info tab displays contact data such as an email address, LinkedIn profile URL, and website URLs. The information that displays here varies based on what these members enter in the Contact Info section on their profiles and whom they allow to view this data (connections only or everyone on LinkedIn).

View this person's contact information

Add your own contact info

Optionally, you can add your own contact info for someone by clicking the Edit Contact Info link, entering your data, and clicking the Done Editing button.

Only you can view contact info you enter for another person.

Manage basic
settings

Access LinkedIn
settings

Select a tab to access
additional settings

In this chapter, you find out how to customize your LinkedIn profile, email, and account settings, including the following:

→ Changing or adding an email address
→ Changing your password
→ Viewing profiles anonymously
→ Customizing email notifications
→ Managing groups and companies you follow
→ Customizing your home page

Customizing Your LinkedIn Settings

Now that you've created a profile and connected with other LinkedIn members, it's time to customize your LinkedIn settings and optimize your experience on the site. If you're not sure which options to choose, selecting the ones that provide you with the most privacy and simplicity while still achieving your goals is a good start.

Customizing the Way You Use LinkedIn

The Account & Settings page provides a lengthy list of options for customizing your LinkedIn experience. On the top part of this page, you can customize LinkedIn's most popular settings, such as your email address and password. The lower part of the page consists of four tabs, enabling you to customize your profile, email notifications, groups, and other account settings.

It's Not All Good

DON'T SKIP ACCOUNT CUSTOMIZATION

The many options provided on the Account & Settings page might seem overwhelming at first, and you might be tempted to skip this step. Setting aside some time to customize the options on this page, often a one-time task, can pay off in the long run.

By customizing your LinkedIn settings, you increase your privacy protection, receive only the specific information you want, and avoid any unpleasant surprises regarding the way LinkedIn handles your personal data.

Open the Account & Settings Page

You can open the Account & Settings page from the navigation bar on any LinkedIn screen. You perform all the tasks in this chapter from this page.

1. Pause your mouse over your photo.

2. Click the Review link.

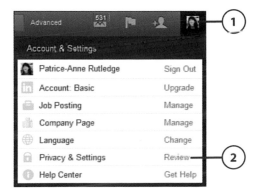

3. Manage basic settings, such as your email address and password.

4. On the Profile tab, customize profile privacy and security settings. This is the default tab; you don't need to click it.

5. Click the Communications tab to manage email notifications.

6. Click the Groups, Companies & Applications tab to manage group settings and the companies you follow.

7. Click the Account tab to manage your account.

Change or Add an Email Address

LinkedIn sends messages to the email address you entered when you signed up for an account. This is called your primary email. You can change your email address at any time or add new email addresses.

1. Click the Change/Add link.

2. Enter a new email address.

3. Click the Add Email Address button.

Confirm Your Email Address

LinkedIn sends you an email confirmation with a link you must click to activate your new address.

4. Click the Remove link next to any email address you want to remove.

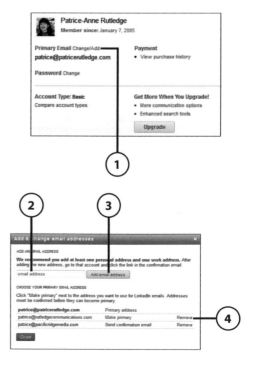

5. Click the Make Primary link to make an email address your primary email.

6. Click the Close button.

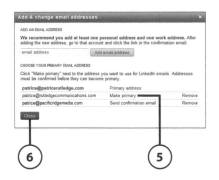

Add All Your Email Addresses

Enter all the email addresses you use in the Add or Change Email Addresses dialog box. This includes your work email, personal email, and school email if you're a recent graduate or still use a university email account. When people invite you to connect, LinkedIn matches the email address they enter for you to your LinkedIn account. Entering all your email accounts helps ensure a match.

Change Your Password

Changing passwords on occasion is a good security measure. Be sure to create a strong password that includes a combination of uppercase and lowercase letters, numbers, and symbols.

1. Click the Change link.

2. Enter your old password.

3. Enter your new password twice.

4. Click the Change Password button.

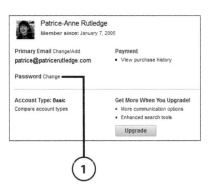

Customizing Profile Settings

The Profile tab of the Account & Settings page enables you to customize your profile settings such as privacy controls. This is the default tab on the Account & Settings page.

Profile tab

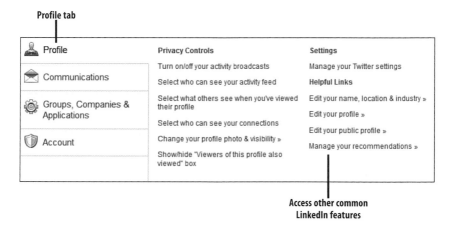

Access other common
LinkedIn features

The Profile Tab

You perform all the tasks in this section on the Profile tab, which displays by default when you open the Account & Settings page. If you're currently using another tab, click the Profile tab to return there.

Manage Your Activity Broadcasts

When you update your status, modify your profile, or make recommendations, LinkedIn broadcasts this activity on the home page of your connections. For most people, this provides good exposure on the LinkedIn network. If you want to block these notifications, however, you can turn them off. For example, you might not want to notify your network of extensive profile changes if you're employed and seeking a new position.

1. Click the Turn On/Off Your Activity Broadcasts link.

2. Remove the check mark to turn off activity broadcasts.

3. Click the Save Changes button.

Turning On Activity Broadcasts

If you decide to turn on activity broadcasts again, return to the Activity Broadcasts dialog box, select the check box, and click the Save Changes button.

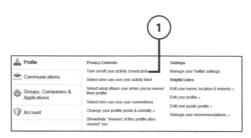

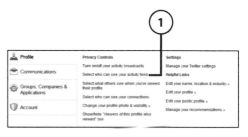

Manage Your Activity Feed

Your activity feed displays on your profile directly below your photo. You can make this feed visible to everyone on LinkedIn or restrict it to only your network or your connections. For maximum privacy, you can choose not to display your activity feed.

1. Click the Select Who Can See Your Activity Feed link.

2. Select your preference from the drop-down list: Everyone, Your Network, Your Connections, or Only You.

3. Click the Save Changes button.

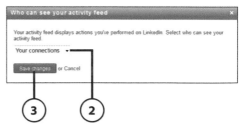

Your Connections Versus Your Network

Your Connections refers to the LinkedIn members you connect with directly. Your Network refers to the people two or three degrees away from your connections (in other words, your connections' connections). See Chapter 6, "Communicating with Other LinkedIn Members," for more information on this distinction.

View Profiles Anonymously

You can customize what, if anything, LinkedIn publishes about you when you visit another member's profile. By default, LinkedIn displays your name and headline. Optionally, you can display anonymous profile characteristics (such as industry and title) or nothing at all. If you're using LinkedIn as a business development tool, you might want others to know you visited their profile. Otherwise, you might prefer complete or partial anonymity.

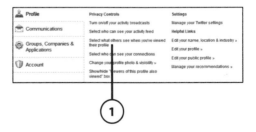

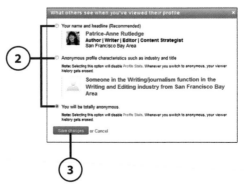

1. Click the Select What Others See When You've Viewed Their Profile link.

2. Select your preference: Your Name and Headline (default setting), Anonymous Profile Characteristics Such as Industry and Title, or You Will Be Totally Anonymous.

3. Click the Save Changes button.

Anonymous Viewing Affects Profile Stats

Be aware that you must allow LinkedIn to display your name and headline to see who's viewed your own profile if you have a free account. If you want to remain anonymous, you must upgrade to a premium account to gain access to this information.

Specify Who Can View Your Connections

By default, LinkedIn allows your direct connections to browse a list of your other connections. This can provide a useful way to develop your network because it's quite likely that you might know some of your con- nections' connections. If you want to hide your connections list, you can choose to do so. Your connections can still view shared connections, however.

1. Click the Select Who Can See Your Connections link.

2. Select your preference: Your Connections or Only You.

3. Click the Save Changes button.

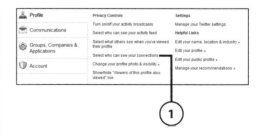

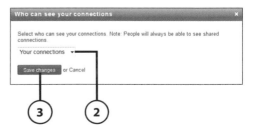

Change Your Profile Photo and Visibility

You can change or remove the photo you uploaded when you created your initial profile. In addition, you can restrict its visibility to only your network or only your connections if you don't want everyone to view your photo. Refer to Chapter 2, "Creating Your LinkedIn Profile," for more information about uploading and editing profile photos.

1. Click the Change Your Profile Photo & Visibility link.

2. Click the Browse button to select a new photo. Depending on your browser or operating system, the name of this button could vary.

3. Click the Upload Photo button to upload your selected photo, replacing any current photo.

4. Specify who can view your photo: My Connections, My Network, or Everyone.

5. Click the Save Settings button.

Crop, Resize, or Delete Your Photo

You can crop or resize your current photo by clicking the Edit Photo link. Clicking the Delete Photo link deletes your current photo.

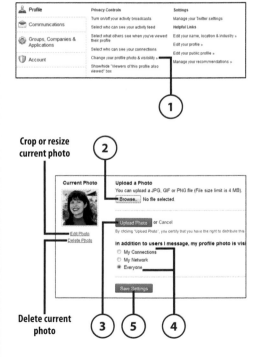

Crop or resize current photo

Delete current photo

Hide Profile Views

By default, LinkedIn displays the
Viewers of This Profile Also Viewed
box on the right side of your profile. This box, which you have the
option to remove, lists other LinkedIn
members whose profiles your profile
viewers have visited. Viewing this
list helps people find other LinkedIn
members to connect with, but it can
also lead them to your competitors.

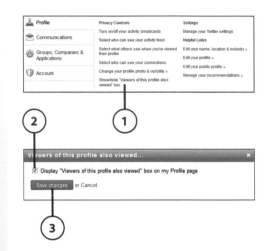

1. Click the Show/Hide "Viewers of
   This Profile Also Viewed" Box link.

2. Remove the check mark to hide
   profile views.

3. Click the Save Changes button.

Manage Your Twitter Settings

When you create your profile,
LinkedIn offers the option to connect it with your Twitter account.
Optionally, you can remove an
enabled Twitter account or add
another Twitter account. Refer to
Chapter 2 for more information
about integrating LinkedIn and
Twitter.

1. Click the Manage Your Twitter
   Settings link.

2. Click the Remove link to remove an enabled Twitter account.

3. Click the Add Another Twitter Account link to add a new Twitter account to your profile.

4. Remove the Account Visibility check mark if you don't want to display your Twitter account on your profile.

5. Click the Save Changes button.

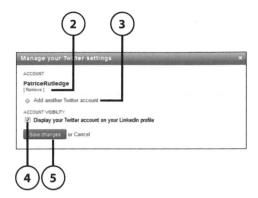

Customizing Email Notification Settings

The Communications tab on the Account & Settings page offers many ways to customize the frequency and type of email notifications that LinkedIn sends you.

Communications Tab Options

On the Communications tab, you can also specify whether you want to receive InMail from LinkedIn's marketing or hiring partners or receive invitations to participate in LinkedIn online market research surveys.

Specify Email Frequency

The Email Frequency page enables you to specify how often you want to receive email updates on each specific communication type LinkedIn offers.

1. Click the Communications tab.

2. Click the Set the Frequency of Emails link.

3. Click the pencil icon to display options for each message type.

4. Specify your email frequency preference for each option: Individual Email, Weekly Digest Email, or No Email.

5. Click the Save Changes button.

Managing Your LinkedIn Messages

Many people choose to receive email notifications for the updates that are most important to them and review online those that are less time-sensitive. For example, you might want to receive invitations and job notifications immediately but review group news only on the Web. If you decide that your choices aren't working well for you, you can always modify these selections.

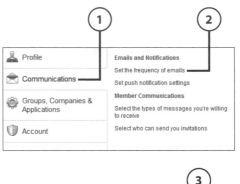

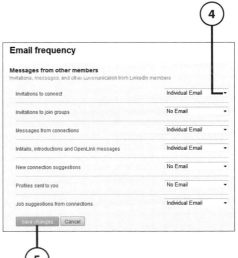

UNDERSTANDING EMAIL FREQUENCY

LinkedIn offers dozens of message types, including messages from other members, connection updates, news, group updates, like and comment notifications, and much more. If you have a large network and belong to numerous groups, all those messages could become overwhelming. Fortunately, LinkedIn enables you to control your email frequency for each message type individually, putting you in control of your email inbox.

You have four choices for the way you receive messages, as follows:

- **Individual Email**—LinkedIn sends an email to your primary email address as soon as the action takes place.

- **Daily Digest Email**—LinkedIn sends one bundled email notification per day. If there is no activity, you don't receive a notification.

- **Weekly Digest Email**—LinkedIn sends one bundled email notification per week. If there is no activity, you don't receive a notification.

- **No Email**—LinkedIn sends no email. You need to go to the LinkedIn website to read messages and notifications.

Not all notification methods are available for each type of message. For example, daily digest emails are available only for group notifications. Additionally, you can't receive network updates by individual email because this would involve more messages than most members want to handle.

Manage Push Notifications

If you access LinkedIn on your mobile device, you can receive messages, invitations to connect, and updates about shares, comments, and likes via push notifications. Fortunately, you can control which notifications you receive.

1. Click the Communications tab.

2. Click the Set Push Notification Settings link.

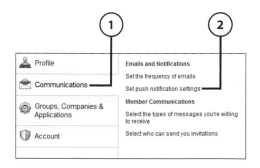

3. Click the pencil icon to display options for each notification type.

4. Remove the check mark next to any notification you don't want to receive.

5. Click the Save Changes button.

Specify the Types of Messages You Want to Receive

You can specify your contact settings, such as whether you're open to receiving InMail and introductions. Refer to Chapter 2 for more information about contact settings.

1. Click the Communications tab.

2. Click the Select the Types of Messages You're Willing to Receive link.

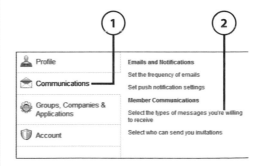

3. Specify whether you want to receive both introductions and InMail (the default) or introductions only.

4. Specify any other opportunities you want to receive, such as career opportunities, job inquiries, consulting offers, and so forth.

5. Update advice for people wanting to contact you.

6. Click the Save Changes button.

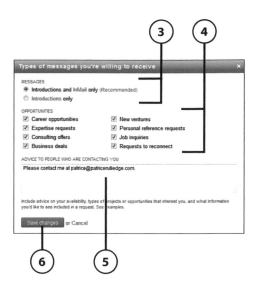

Specify Who Can Send You Invitations

By default, LinkedIn sends you all invitations, but you can choose to receive invitations only from those who know your email address or those who are in your Imported Contacts list (such as people who are in your Gmail or Outlook contacts). See Chapter 3, "Developing Your LinkedIn Network," to learn more about contact lists.

It's Not All Good

DON'T BE TOO CAREFUL

Keep in mind that restricting your invitations could block an invitation from someone you might actually want to connect with. Being open to all invitations leads to the most opportunities on LinkedIn. If you receive an invitation from someone you don't want to connect with, you don't have to accept.

1. Click the Communications tab.

2. Click the Select Who Can Send You Invitations link.

3. Specify your invitation preference: Anyone on LinkedIn (the default), Only People Who Know Your Email Address or Appear in Your "Imported Contacts" List, or Only People Who Appear in Your "Imported Contacts" List.

4. Click the Save Changes button.

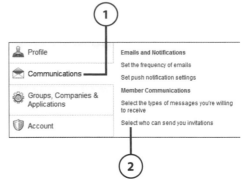

Managing Group, Company, and Application Settings

The Groups, Companies & Applications tab on the Account & Settings page enables you to customize your settings for groups, LinkedIn Company Pages, and applications.

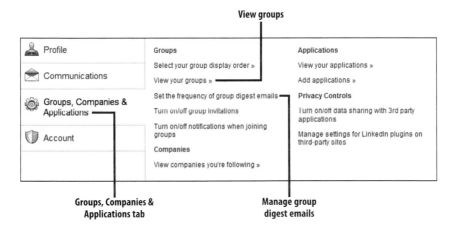

Specify Group Display Order

You can specify the order in which groups display on the Your Groups page. See Chapter 14, "Participating in LinkedIn Groups," for more information on creating and using LinkedIn groups.

1. Click the Groups, Companies & Applications tab.

2. Click the Select Your Group Display Order link.

3. Use the Order field to move each of your groups up or down until you reach your desired display order.

Change Group Settings

You can specify different settings for each of your groups. Click the Member Settings link to make changes to a particular group. See "Managing Group Settings" in Chapter 14 for more information.

4. Click the Save Changes button. (If you have numerous groups, you might have to scroll to the bottom of the page).

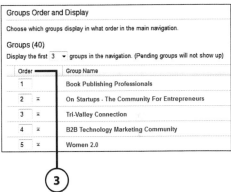

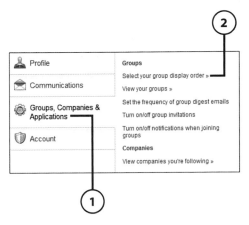

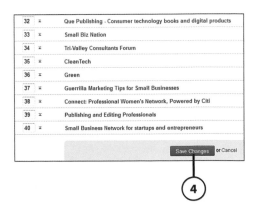

Turn Off Group Invitations

By default, LinkedIn sends you group invitations from your connections. If you don't want to receive these invitations, you can block them.

1. Click the Groups, Companies & Applications tab.

2. Click the Turn On/Off Group Invitations link.

3. Remove the check mark in the Group Invitations dialog box.

4. Click the Save Changes button.

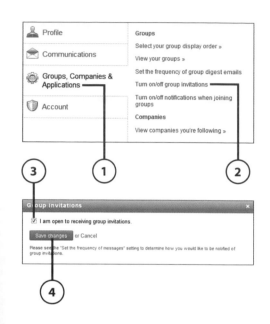

Turn Off Group Notifications

LinkedIn publishes an update to your network when you join a group with notifications enabled. If you don't want to announce the groups you join, you can block these notifications. For example, you might not want to tell the world you're joining a job search group if you're still employed.

1. Click the Groups, Companies & Applications tab.

2. Click the Turn On/Off Notifications When Joining Groups link.

3. Remove the check mark in the Notifications When Joining Groups dialog box.

4. Click the Save Changes button.

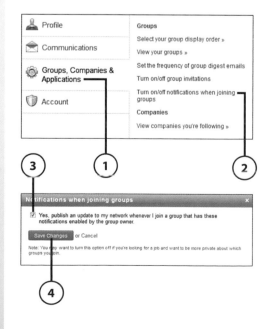

View Companies You're Following

You can view a list of the companies you're following and stop following selected companies. See Chapter 15, "Working with Company Pages," for more information about following companies.

1. Click the Groups, Companies & Applications tab.

2. Click the View Companies You're Following link.

3. Click a company name to view its LinkedIn company page.

4. Click the Stop Following link to stop following a company.

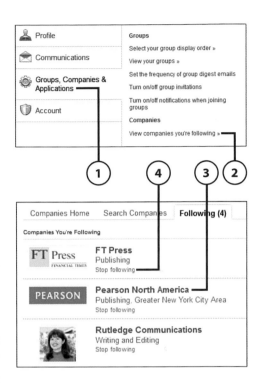

Manage Applications That Access LinkedIn

Some third-party applications request that you grant them access to your LinkedIn account when you sign up or use certain features. For example, if you use websites such as SlideShare, Klout, or Scoop.it, you could have granted access to LinkedIn. If you decide you no longer want an application to have access to your account, you can remove it.

1. Click the Groups, Companies & Applications tab.

2. Click the View Your Applications link.

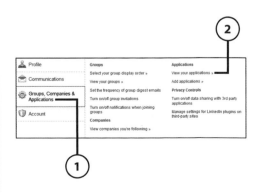

3. Select the check box next to any applications you want to remove.

4. Click the Remove button.

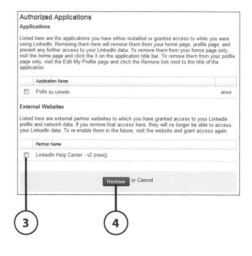

Manage Data Sharing with Third-Party Applications

By default, LinkedIn shares some of your data with third-party applications. Optionally, you can turn off this feature.

LinkedIn's Privacy Policy

To learn more about LinkedIn's privacy policy, click the Privacy Policy link on the bottom menu. See section 2.G of the policy for details about third-party data sharing.

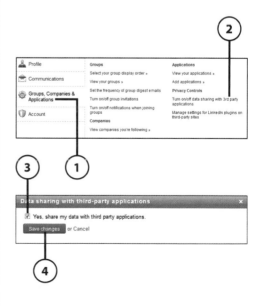

1. Click the Groups, Companies & Applications tab.

2. Click the Turn On/Off Data Sharing with 3rd Party Applications link.

3. Remove the check mark in the dialog box.

4. Click the Save Changes button.

Manage LinkedIn Plugins on Third-Party Sites

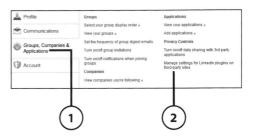

If you're logged in to LinkedIn, it receives notification when you visit third-party sites that use LinkedIn plugins. Optionally, you can turn off this feature.

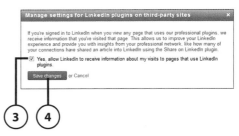

1. Click the Groups, Companies & Applications tab.

2. Click the Manage Settings for LinkedIn Plugins on Third-Party Sites link.

3. Remove the check mark in the dialog box.

4. Click the Save Changes button.

Managing Your Account Settings

The Account tab on the Account & Settings page enables you to manage privacy controls, upgrade your account, subscribe to LinkedIn content via RSS, and modify other settings. This tab also includes links to features you can access in other parts of LinkedIn.

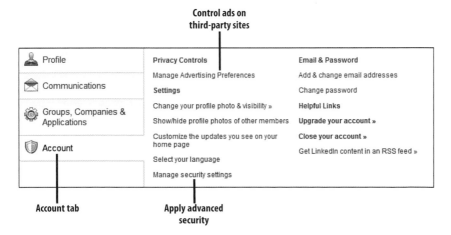

Customize Your Home Page Updates

Network updates on your home page give you a quick snapshot of your connections' activities on LinkedIn. For example, the home page displays updates about new connections, job opportunities, profile changes, trending news, group activity, and news from companies you follow. Although it's good to keep up with what's new in your network, you might find that some updates are more interesting than others are. Fortunately, there's a way to customize exactly what appears on your home page.

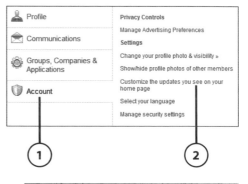

1. Click the Account tab.

2. Click the Customize the Updates You See on Your Home Page link.

3. Remove the check mark next to any updates you don't want to display.

4. Specify how many updates you want on your home page: 10, 15, 20, or 25. The default is 15.

5. Click the Save Changes button.

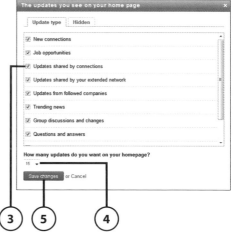

Close Your Account

If for any reason you no longer want to use LinkedIn, you can close your account.

1. Click the Account tab.

2. Click the Close Your Account link.

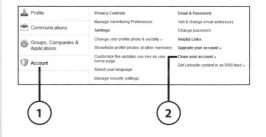

3. Select your reason for closing your account.

4. Click the Continue button.

5. Click the Verify Account button to confirm that you want to close your account.

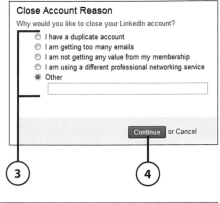

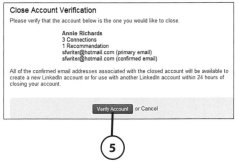

It's Not All Good

THINK CAREFULLY BEFORE CLOSING

Keep in mind that if you close your account, you lose all your LinkedIn connections and no longer have access to the site. If your reason for closing is because you're concerned about privacy or receive too many unwanted communications, review the options in this chapter first. You might discover that you can resolve your concerns without losing a professional network you could need in the future.

Get LinkedIn Content in an RSS Feed

If you use a feed reader such as FeedDemon or Netvibes to subscribe to and read your favorite blogs and news feeds, you might be interested in adding your LinkedIn feed. On the LinkedIn RSS Feeds page, you can subscribe to a private feed of the network updates that display on your home page.

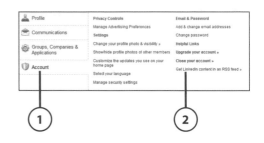

1. Click the Account tab.

2. Click the Get LinkedIn Content in an RSS Feed link.

3. Select the Enable option button.

4. Select your feed reader.

Where's My Feed Reader?

If your preferred reader isn't among the options on the LinkedIn RSS Feeds page, you can use the RSS link in another reader.

>>>Go Further

UNDERSTANDING RSS

RSS stands for Really Simple Syndication, a popular format for web feeds. Content publishers can syndicate their content with a feed, making it available for users to subscribe to and view with feed reader applications. Feeds for blog content are most common, but you can also create a feed for web content such as the content on LinkedIn.

The advantage of feeds is that you can view frequently updated content from your favorite blogs, podcasts, news sites, and other websites in one place. The standard feed icon is a small orange square with white radio waves, letting you know that the content is available via feed for your subscription.

It's Not All Good

ENSURING FEED PRIVACY

It's important to understand the difference between a private feed and a public feed. LinkedIn private feeds contain personal data such as your updates and your connections' updates and are meant for your private viewing.

Public feeds contain data available for public viewing on the Web. Be careful not to publish your private feed on the Web. If you use a web-based feed reader, verify that your data will remain private if you don't want others to view your LinkedIn network updates.

Profile updates
on a home page

 Say congrats on the new job!

 Sara Wretstrom
Account Manager
Tipford PR

Like · Say congrats · 2h ago

 Annie Richards

Just signed a new client I've wanted to work with for a long time. Very excited!

Like · Comment · Share · 9h ago

 Patrice-Anne Rutledge's skills and expertise were endorsed by Anne Rutledge.

Patrice-Anne was endorsed for Content Strategy and New Media.

Endorse your connections · 2d ago

A shared
update

In this chapter, you find out how to maintain a solid presence on LinkedIn by updating your profile consistently and sharing strategic updates with your network, including:

→ Updating your profile
→ Sharing a text update
→ Sharing a link
→ Sharing an attached file
→ Deleting an update

Managing and Updating Your Profile

Keeping active is critical to your success on LinkedIn. Creating your initial profile might be a one-time task, but you need to update it regularly to let others know you're an active participant on LinkedIn. In addition to updating your actual profile, LinkedIn enables you to post frequent status updates to inform your network about your activities and accomplishments.

Maintaining an Updated Profile

Even if you create a thorough profile when you first sign up for LinkedIn, you need to update it regularly with new content. For example, you should update your LinkedIn profile whenever your employment status changes, you receive a degree or certification, win an award, learn a new skill, start a new business, achieve a career milestone, or change your LinkedIn goals.

Update Your Profile

You update your profile on the Edit Profile page. This is where you first created your profile, so you should already be familiar with its content. For a reminder of how to enter profile content, see Chapter 2, "Creating Your LinkedIn Profile."

1. Select Edit Profile from the Profile drop-down menu.

2. Click the Edit link next to the content you want to update. In this example, you edit a position.

3. Edit your selected content.

4. Click the Save button.

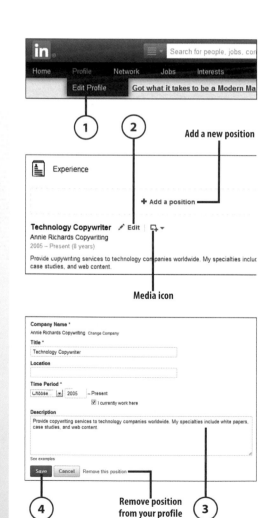

5. Click the Done Editing button.

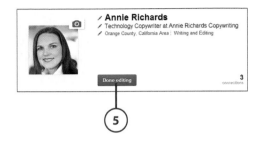

Updating Other Content

Although the Edit link is the most common way to edit profile content, you can also pause your mouse over the media icon to insert or upload media content or click a descriptive link such as Add a Position or Add Education. See Chapter 2 for more details about adding content to your LinkedIn profile, including media content.

It's Not All Good

DON'T LET YOUR PROFILE GET OUTDATED

Although it's not necessary to update your profile every week, you shouldn't let it get outdated either. If it's obvious you haven't touched your profile in months—or years—LinkedIn members might not bother contacting you for what could have been a lucrative opportunity for you.

>>>Go Further

UNDERSTANDING WHERE LINKEDIN DISPLAYS YOUR PROFILE UPDATES

LinkedIn announces your profile updates in several places:

- On your home page.

- On your connections' home pages. This occurs only if you turned on activity broadcasts on the Profile tab of the Account & Settings page and if your connections haven't removed profile changes from their home pages on the Account tab of the Account & Settings page.

- In your connections' email updates. This occurs only for new positions and only if your connections opted to receive network updates via email on the Communications tab of the Account & Settings page. LinkedIn doesn't email your connections about minor profile changes.

See Chapter 4, "Customizing Your LinkedIn Settings," for more information about the Account & Settings page.

Sharing Updates

LinkedIn enables you to share important news with other LinkedIn members in the Share an Update box on your home page or your profile. You can share a basic text update of up to 600 characters; a link title, description, and optional photo; and an external file you attach.

It's Not All Good

FOLLOW LINKEDIN UPDATE ETIQUETTE

Although updates are a good way to let your connections know what's new in your life, they are also a strategic networking tool. Keep your goals in mind and post updates that help achieve them. A well-crafted update can be an effective marketing and publicity tool, but be careful to avoid overt sales pitches in your updates. An update is a conversation with your network, not an advertisement.

In addition, LinkedIn isn't the place for excessive updates. Unlike Twitter, where sharing multiple times a day is common and accepted, sharing updates several times a week is sufficient on LinkedIn.

Share a Text Update

You can share a basic text update on your home page or profile.

1. Type your update in the Share an Update box.

2. Select who you want to share with: everyone on LinkedIn, everyone on LinkedIn and Twitter, or only your connections.

3. Click the Share button.

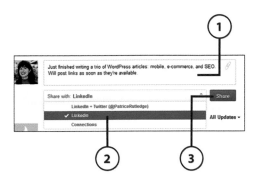

Mention People and Companies

Optionally, you can mention your connections or companies with a LinkedIn Company Page in your LinkedIn updates. To do so, type @ and then the person or company name. LinkedIn helps you by displaying a list of potential matches as you type. When you mention a person or company, this name becomes a link that others can preview or click.

Start typing a name

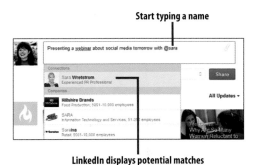

LinkedIn displays potential matches

Share a Link

You can share a link on your home page or profile. For example, you could share your latest blog post or an interesting article you read on the Web.

1. Enter your link in the Share an Update box along with any text you want to include.

2. Click the title or description box to make any changes.

Select an image

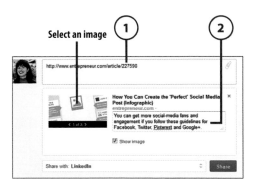

3. The Show Image check box is selected by default. Remove this check mark if you don't want to include a photo.

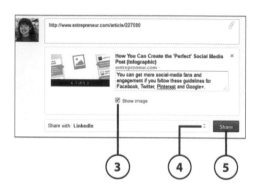

Selecting an Image

Some content you link to could have more than one image option. To change from the default image, click the arrows below it to view alternative selections. LinkedIn searches for any images on the page you're sharing and offers them as options.

4. Select who you want to share with: everyone on LinkedIn, everyone on LinkedIn and Twitter, or only your connections.

5. Click the Share button.

Share an Attached File

You can share a file with your LinkedIn network on your home page or profile. For example, you could share an image, Word file, presentation, or PDF stored on your computer or another network location.

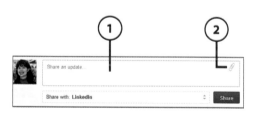

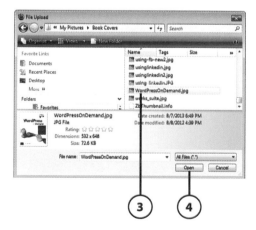

1. Type your update in the Share an Update box.

2. Click the Attach a File icon.

3. Select your file.

4. Click the Open button. Depending on your browser and operating system, this button might have a different name.

5. Select who you want to share with: everyone on LinkedIn, everyone on LinkedIn and Twitter, or only your connections.

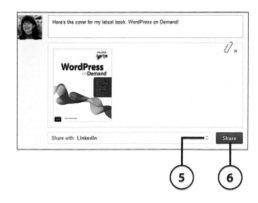

Renaming a Title and Description

If you attach a file that includes a title and description, such as a Word document or PDF, you can edit this data.

6. Click the Share button.

SHARING ON TWITTER

LinkedIn gives you the option of sharing your updates with your connections, everyone on LinkedIn, or everyone on LinkedIn plus Twitter. If you want to share your LinkedIn updates on Twitter, you should limit them to 140 characters. Otherwise, Twitter cuts off the remaining content in your tweet.

If you haven't already linked your LinkedIn account to Twitter, LinkedIn prompts you to do so when you select the LinkedIn + Twitter sharing option. Refer to Chapter 2 for more information about integrating LinkedIn and Twitter.

UNDERSTANDING WHERE LINKEDIN DISPLAYS YOUR SHARED UPDATES

When you share an update, it displays in several places:

- On your home page.

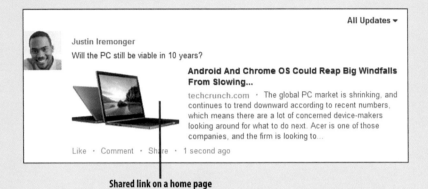

Shared link on a home page

- On your connections' home pages. This occurs only if you turned on activity broadcasts on the Profile tab of the Account & Settings page and if your connections haven't removed updates from their home pages on the Account tab of the Account & Settings page.

View your recent LinkedIn activity and updates

Delete an update

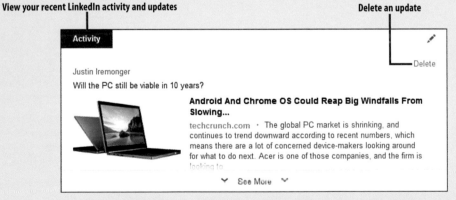

- In the Activity section of your own Edit Profile page, just below your name and headline.

- In the Activity section of your profile page (the one other LinkedIn members see), just below your name and headline. This occurs only if you enabled others to view your activity feed on the Profile tab of the Account & Settings page.

Delete an Update on Your Home Page

Although you can delete updates from the Activity section of your profile, you can also delete updates on your home page.

Delete Versus Hide

Be aware that you can delete only your own updates. If you no longer want to see updates from a connection, pause your mouse over one of this person's updates and click the Hide link.

1. If you aren't already on your home page, click the Home link.

2. If your update isn't visible on the home page, select Your Updates from the All Updates drop-down list.

3. Pause your mouse over your update and click the Delete link.

4. Click the Delete button in the confirmation dialog box.

UNDERSTANDING HOW YOUR NETWORK CAN RESPOND TO YOUR UPDATE

When your update appears on your connections' home page, they can do the following:

- Show their support for your update by clicking the Like link. Your number of likes displays in parentheses after the Like link.

- Add a comment by clicking the Comment link below your update. If your connections have entered comments about your update, you see a link beneath your posted update on your home page and on your profile. The number of comments you have is displayed in parentheses after the Comments link—for example, Comments (2). Click this link to view your comments and add your own feedback to the discussion.

- Share your update with their connections or fellow group members or in updates of their own by clicking the Share link.

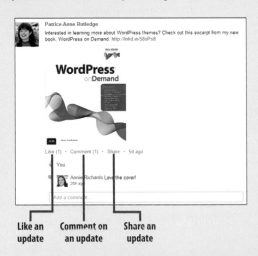

Like an update   Comment on an update   Share an update

See Chapter 9, "Viewing News on LinkedIn," for more information about interacting with LinkedIn updates.

View messages   View invitations   Filter your messages

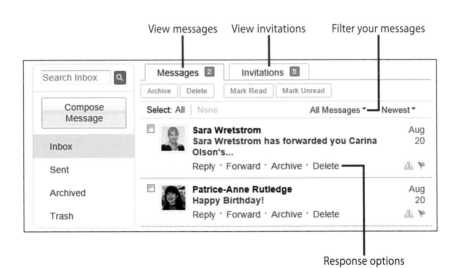

Response options

In this chapter, you learn about the LinkedIn network and the many ways to communicate with other LinkedIn members.

→ Sending a message from the inbox
→ Sending a message from a profile
→ Sending InMail to an OpenLink Network participant
→ Managing your inbox
→ Requesting introductions

Communicating with Other LinkedIn Members

LinkedIn is based on connection and communication between its members. Fortunately, you have several options for staying in touch with the people you know and reaching out to new people, including messages, InMail, and introductions.

Understanding LinkedIn Messages, InMail, and Introductions

LinkedIn offers several ways to communicate with other members. The type of communication you can send depends on how you're connected to these members. Your choices include the following:

- **Messages**— Messages are the primary form of communication on LinkedIn. You can send messages only to your 1st degree connections or to group members (directly from a group, not from their profiles). See the "Sending Messages" section later in this chapter for more information. Although you often see the term *message* used generically to refer to all items in your inbox, it is a specific type of communication in itself.

You can send a message to this
1st degree connection

- **Invitations**—An invitation is a request to connect with another LinkedIn member. Refer to Chapter 3, "Developing Your LinkedIn Network," for more information about sending invitations.

- **InMail**—An InMail is a private message to or from a LinkedIn member who is not your connection. You can receive InMail if you indicate that you are open to receiving InMail messages on the Account & Settings page. In general, sending InMail is a paid LinkedIn feature unless the recipient is a premium member who belongs to the OpenLink Network. See the "Sending InMail" section later in this chapter for more information.

You can send free InMail to this
OpenLink Network participant

- **Introductions**—An introduction provides a way to reach out to the people who are connected to your connections. By requesting an introduction through someone you already know, that person can introduce you to the person you're trying to reach. You can contact your 1st degree connections to request introductions to members who are 2nd and 3rd degree connections. Members with free accounts can have up to five introductions open at a time. See the "Requesting Introductions" section later in this chapter for more information.

Managing Your Inbox

Your inbox is the focal point for all your direct communication on LinkedIn.

Preview Your Inbox

LinkedIn makes it easy to preview what's new in your inbox from anywhere on its site.

1. Pause over the Inbox button on the navigation bar.

2. LinkedIn displays a list of your most recent invitations and messages.

3. Click an invitation to view the sender's profile.

4. Pause over an invitation to accept or ignore it.

5. Click a message to open it.

6. Pause over a message to reply to it or delete it.

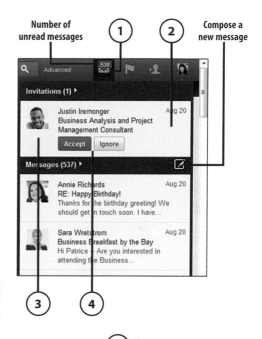

Number of unread messages ① ② Compose a new message

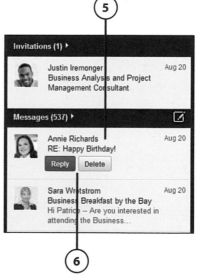

View Messages in Your Inbox

The default view of your inbox is the Messages tab, which displays all the messages you've received. If you have a lot of inbox messages, you can filter what displays: only unread messages, flagged messages, InMails, recommendations, introductions, profiles, jobs, or blocked messages. By default, LinkedIn displays your messages in order from newest to oldest.

Viewing Invitations

The inbox also includes another tab: Invitations. This tab displays all open invitations you need to respond to. Refer to Chapter 3 for more information about responding to invitations to connect.

1. Click the Inbox button on the navigation bar.

2. View a message by clicking its subject line.

3. Click the All Messages link and choose one of the available options from the drop-down menu to filter your messages by topic.

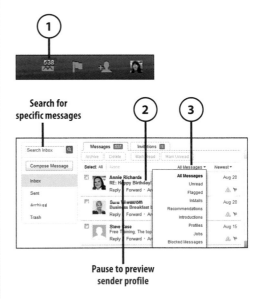

Search for specific messages

Pause to preview sender profile

Searching for Specific Content

In addition to filtering inbox items, you can search for a specific message. Enter a keyword in the Search Inbox box on the left side of the page and click the Search button (the button with the magnifying glass). LinkedIn displays all messages containing that search term. For example, you could search for a person's name or a word or phrase in the subject line or message text.

4. By default, LinkedIn displays your messages in order from newest to oldest. To reverse this order, click the Newest link and select Oldest.

5. Click the Flag icon, which acts as a toggle, to flag or unflag a message for follow-up.

6. Click the Report Spam icon to notify LinkedIn of a spam message.

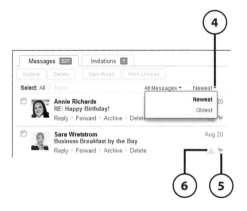

Reply to a Message

In addition to replying to messages from the inbox preview, you can send replies directly from the inbox.

1. Click the Reply link below the message to which you want to reply.

You can also forward a message

2. Enter your response in the text box.

3. Select the Send Me a Copy check box if you want LinkedIn to email you a copy of your message.

4. Click the Send Message button.

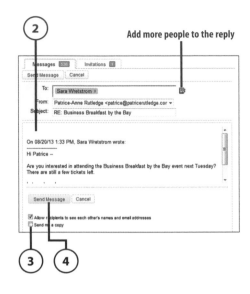

Add more people to the reply

Archive Messages

It's a good idea to archive old or resolved messages to keep your inbox focused on your current action items. When you archive a message, LinkedIn moves it the Archived folder.

1. Click the Archive link below the message you want to archive.

2. To archive multiple messages, select the check boxes to their left and click the Archive button.

3. Click the Archived tab to view archived messages.

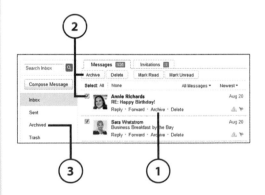

Mark and Unmark Messages as Read

LinkedIn marks messages in your inbox as read or unread so that you can keep track of what needs your attention. By default, new messages appear in bold text to signify that you haven't read them (unread status). After you read a message, the message no longer is boldfaced in your inbox (read status). You can change the status of messages manually if you prefer.

1. Select the check box to the left of the messages whose read status you want to change.

2. Click the Mark Read button to change the message status to read.

3. Click the Mark Unread button to change the message status to unread.

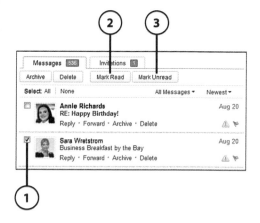

Delete Messages

You can delete unwanted messages from your inbox and move them to your Trash folder. In this folder, you can choose to empty your trash, undelete a message you deleted by mistake, or delete messages permanently.

1. Click the Delete link below a message you want to delete.

2. To delete multiple messages, select the check boxes to their left and click the Delete button.

3. Click the Trash tab to view deleted messages.

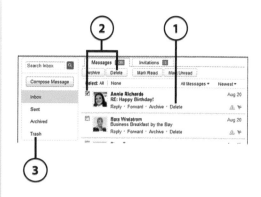

4. Click the Undelete link below a message you want to undelete. LinkedIn returns it to your inbox.

5. Click the Delete Permanently link below a message you want to delete permanently.

You Can Archive or Delete Multiple Messages

To undelete or permanently delete more than one message at a time, select the check boxes to the left of all targeted messages and then click either the Undelete or Delete Permanently button at the top of the inbox.

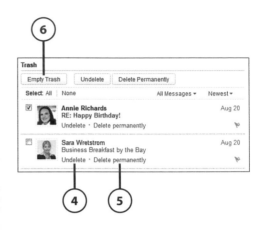

6. Click the Empty Trash button to delete all messages permanently.

Sending Messages

LinkedIn offers numerous ways to send messages, including sending messages from the inbox or from a member's profile.

Send a Message from the Inbox

One way to send a message to one of your 1st degree connections is from your inbox.

1. Click the Compose Message button.

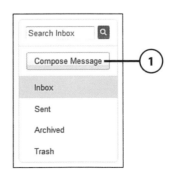

2. Start typing the name of the person you want to message. As you type, LinkedIn displays potential matches you can select.

Send a Message to Multiple Connections

Alternatively, click the address book icon to open your connection list. With the address book, you can search for the person you want to reach or select multiple recipients for your message. LinkedIn enables you to send a message to up to 50 connections at one time.

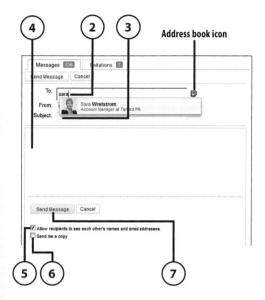

Address book icon

3. Enter a subject for your message.

4. Enter your message in the text box.

5. If you're sending a message to multiple recipients and don't want to disclose this information, remove the check mark before the Allow Recipients to See Each Other's Names and Email Addresses check box (selected by default).

6. To email yourself a copy of your message, select the Send Me a Copy check box. Your message already appears in your Sent folder by default.

7. Click the Send Message button.

Send a Message from a Connection's Profile

You can also send a message to your 1st degree connections from their profiles.

Finding a Profile

The easiest way to find someone's profile is by using the search box at the top of the LinkedIn screen. See Chapter 7, "Searching on LinkedIn," for more information about the search box.

1. Click the Send a Message button.

2. Enter a subject for your message.

3. Enter your message in the text box.

4. Click the Send Message button.

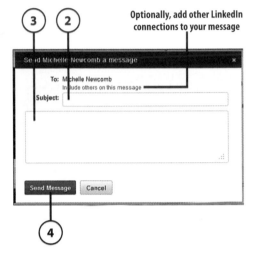

Optionally, add other LinkedIn connections to your message

OTHER WAYS TO MESSAGE YOUR LINKEDIN CONNECTIONS

Although sending your connections a message from your inbox or from their profiles is common, LinkedIn offers several other ways to message your connections. You can also do the following:

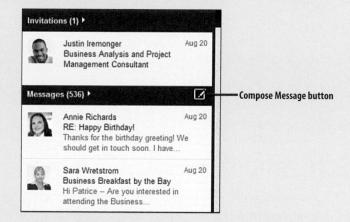

Compose Message button

- Pause over the Inbox button on the navigation bar and click the Compose Message button.

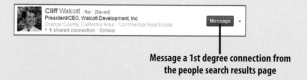

Message a 1st degree connection from the people search results page

- Click the Message button in people search results. This button displays only next to people who are your 1st degree connections. See Chapter 7 for more information about people search results.

Message a connection from your home page

- Pause over a connection's name on your home page and click the Send a Message button in the profile preview.

A connection's external contact information

Contacting people off of LinkedIn is another option. The profiles of your 1st degree connections display their external email addresses in the Contact Info tab below their headlines and photos. In addition, some members include their email addresses directly on their profiles for the entire LinkedIn network to see.

Sending InMail

As mentioned earlier in this chapter, InMail enables you to contact LinkedIn members who aren't in your network. In an effort to manage spam, LinkedIn requires members to pay to send InMail. InMail is most useful for members who want to contact a wide variety of people, such as recruiters or individuals using LinkedIn for business development.

There is one exception in which you can send InMail for free, even if you don't have a premium account: You can send InMail at no charge to members who participate in the OpenLink Network. LinkedIn identifies these members with the OpenLink icon on their profiles or in search results. To enable other members to send *you* free InMail, you must specify that you want to participate in the OpenLink Network when you sign up for a premium account.

>>Go Further

INMAIL UPGRADE OPTIONS

LinkedIn premium accounts, including Job Seeker premium accounts, enable you to send a fixed number of InMail messages per month. To learn more about LinkedIn premium accounts and InMail, click the Upgrade link on the navigation menu.

You can also purchase individual InMails at $10 each by pausing over your photo in the upper-right corner of the screen and selecting Review. Then click the Purchase link below the InMails field on the Account & Settings page. This is cost-efficient only if you want to contact just a few people by InMail.

Refer to Chapter 1, "Introducing LinkedIn," to learn more about premium account options. See Chapter 10, "Finding a Job," to learn more about Job Seeker premium accounts.

You can purchase individual InMails

Send InMail to an OpenLink Network Participant

You can send free InMail to participants in the OpenLink Network directly from their profile. If the recipient doesn't respond to the InMail within seven days, the message expires.

1. Verify that the person you want to contact is an OpenLink Network participant.

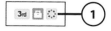

Why Can't I Send InMail?

Remember that you can send free InMail only to OpenLink Network members. If you click the Send InMail link on the profile of another member, LinkedIn prompts you to sign up for a premium account if you don't already have one.

2. Click the Send InMail link on the profile of the person you want to reach.

3. Enter your email address and phone number if you want to share contact information.

Hiding Contact Information

If you don't want to share your contact information with the person you want to reach, remove the check mark from the Include My Contact Information check box (selected by default). In general, it's a good idea to share contact information.

4. Select the reason for your InMail, such as job inquiry or business opportunity.

5. Enter the subject of your InMail.

6. Enter your message. To increase your chances of a positive reply, be as specific as possible.

7. Click the Send button to send your InMail.

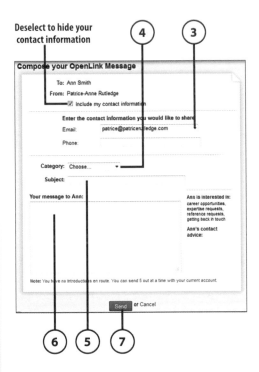

Deselect to hide your contact information

Consider Alternatives to InMail

Although InMail is an effective LinkedIn communication tool, it comes at a price. If you want to contact someone you don't know and don't want to pay to send InMail, you have several other options. You could join a group that this person belongs to and then send a message or invitation to connect as a fellow group member. You could also request an introduction through a mutual connection. Alternatively, you could choose to contact the individual outside LinkedIn by accessing the website links and external email information that individuals provide on their profiles.

Requesting Introductions

Requesting an introduction is a good way to connect with people in your network with whom you don't connect directly. Although you can send an invitation to someone you don't know, you might want to consider requesting an introduction through a shared connection for important communications. An introduction can carry more weight than a cold contact.

For example, let's say that you're connected to your former manager, Felice (1st degree connection), who is connected to Dalton (2nd degree connection), a manager at another local company. You're interested in working in Dalton's department, but you don't know him and haven't seen any posted job openings. Rather than sending Dalton an email and resume as a cold contact, you could send an introduction request through Felice.

Often you already know how you're connected to the person you want to reach, but you can also determine this by viewing the How You're Connected section in the right column of your target contact's profile. If you don't already know of a common connection, this section could list a name you recognize.

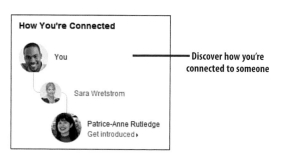

Discover how you're connected to someone

>>>Go Further

MAKING THE MOST OF LINKEDIN INTRODUCTIONS

Here are several tips for making the most of LinkedIn introductions:

- **Talk to your 1st degree connection before sending an introduction request on LinkedIn**—Your connection might have information that's pertinent to your request. For example, if you're trying to reach someone about job opportunities, your connection might know whether your target is hiring or whether there's a more suitable person to contact.

- **Make your introduction request concise and specific**—A vague request to "get to know" someone isn't nearly as effective as stating your specific purpose, such as seeking employment, recruiting for a job, offering consulting services, and so forth.

- **Keep in mind that LinkedIn provides only five introductions per month with a free basic account**—You can find out how many introductions you still have available on the Account & Settings page (pause over your photo on the navigation menu and select Review from the menu). To increase your number of open introductions, you need to upgrade to a premium account. LinkedIn recommends using introductions judiciously rather than as a tool to contact hundreds of members.

It's Not All Good

FOCUS ON INTRODUCTIONS TO 2ND DEGREE CONNECTIONS

Although a 2nd degree connection can request an introduction to a 3rd degree connection, this requires two intermediaries. In many cases, the second intermediary (your 2nd degree connection passing on your request to your 3rd degree connection) probably doesn't know you and could be less inclined to forward your introduction. For best results, focus on introductions to 2nd degree connections rather than 3rd degree connections.

Request an Introduction

The easiest way to request an introduction is through your target contact's profile.

1. Click the down arrow to the right of the Send InMail button and select Get Introduced.

Where's the Get Introduced Link?

Remember that the Get Introduced link displays only for people who are your 2nd or 3rd degree connections. If someone is outside your network, you can only send that person InMail or invite him to connect.

2. Select the person from whom you want to request the introduction. If you have only one connection in common with the individual you want to reach, only that connection displays in this box.

3. Enter the subject of your request.

4. Enter a message to the person you want to be introduced to. It's also a good idea to add a brief note to the person you want to make the referral (your 1st degree connection).

5. Click the Send Request button to send your introduction request.

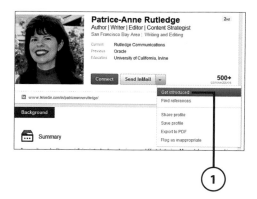

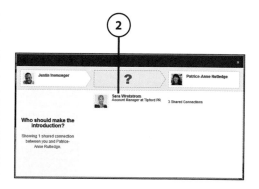

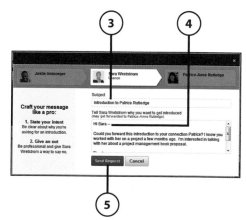

Another Way to Request an Introduction

You can also request an introduction by clicking the down arrow to the right of the Connect button in people search results and selecting Get Introduced. See Chapter 7 for more information about searching for people.

What Happens Next?

Your 1st degree connection receives your request and can choose to forward it to your target connection with comments or decline your request. If your request wasn't clear, your connection might ask you for more information. See the following section, "Manage Introduction Requests," for more information about the next step in the process.

Request an introduction from people search results

Manage Introduction Requests

In addition to requesting your own introductions to others, you might receive introduction requests in your inbox. For example, LinkedIn members might ask you to facilitate an introduction to one of your connections or might ask your connection to facilitate an introduction to you.

1. Click the All Messages link in your inbox and select Introductions from the drop-down menu.

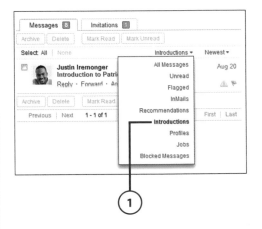

2. Click the subject line link.

3. Click the Forward button to forward the request to your connection.

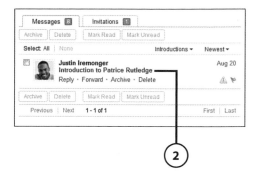

Declining an Introduction Request

If you don't want to make the introduction, click the Decline button, select a reason why you feel the introduction isn't a good fit, and click the Send button. The person who requested the introduction receives your feedback on why you declined the introduction.

4. Enter any additional comments about this introduction request.

5. Click the Forward Message button.

What Happens Next?

The target recipient receives your forwarded introduction request and can accept or decline it. Accepting the introduction enables the requestor and target to communicate with each other, but they still need to send an invitation request to become connections.

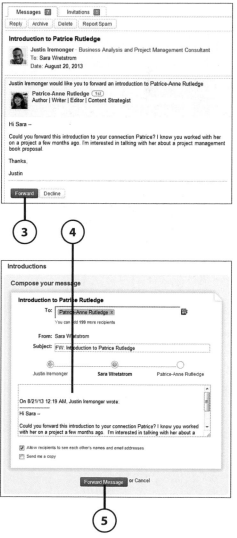

Refine your search   Quick search box   Advanced search

People search results

In this chapter, you explore LinkedIn quick searches, people searches, and advanced search techniques. Topics include:

→ Performing a quick search

→ Searching for a specific person

→ Viewing people search results

→ Interacting with people on the search results page

→ Narrowing people search results

→ Performing an advanced people search

→ Saving a people search

Searching on LinkedIn

LinkedIn is a large, complex network of information. You can greatly improve your chances of achieving your networking goals by knowing how to find exactly what you want among millions of member profiles, company pages, jobs, group discussions, and other data.

This chapter focuses on quick searches and searching for people. To learn more about searching for jobs, companies, and groups or searching your Inbox, refer to the chapters in this book that cover those topics.

Finding Information Fast on LinkedIn

LinkedIn makes it easy to find information about people, jobs, companies, groups, and more from any page on its site.

Perform a Quick Search

The easiest way to search for information on LinkedIn is to use the quick search box on LinkedIn's navigation bar.

1. Select the focus of your search from the drop-down list.

2. Enter your search term. This might be a person's name, company name, job title, or job skill, for example.

3. Click the Search button.

4. LinkedIn displays matching search results. The format of the search results depends on the type of search you perform.

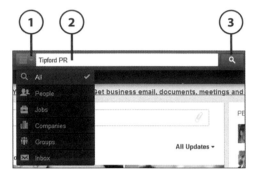

Searching for People

Searching for people is by far the most common LinkedIn search. LinkedIn offers several ways to find exactly who you're looking for, whether it's someone you already know (such as a former colleague or classmate) or someone who matches very specific criteria (such as accountants in Indianapolis or engineers who formerly worked for Google).

Search for a Specific Person

The fastest way to search for a specific person is to perform a quick search.

1. Enter the name of the person you want to find.

2. As you type, LinkedIn displays a drop-down list of potential matches. If you see a match in this list, click that person's name to open the corresponding profile.

3. If you don't see a match, click the Search button to display a detailed list of potential matches.

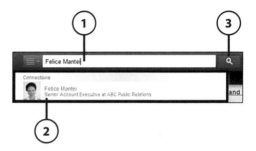

View People Search Results

Each LinkedIn member who matches your search results appears in a preview box that includes a photo, name, headline, location, industry, and information about shared connections and groups. Depending on the preview you're viewing, not all items might appear. For example, a member might choose not to upload or display a photo.

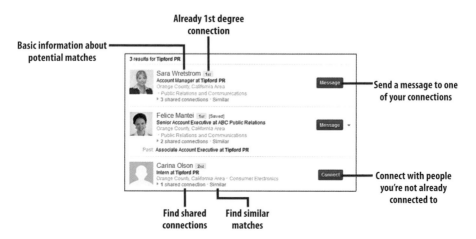

Already 1st degree connection

Basic information about potential matches

Send a message to one of your connections

Connect with people you're not already connected to

Find shared connections   Find similar matches

Search Results Limits

With a personal account, you can view 100 results at a time. To view more results, you need to upgrade to a premium account. To learn more about premium accounts, click the Upgrade link on the navigation bar.

Icons appear to the right of LinkedIn member names indicating their connection to you, such as a 1st degree connection, 2nd degree connection, 3rd degree connection, or group member. For members who are out of your network, you might see the Out of Your Network designation next to their names, or their names might be hidden from view. If your own name appears in search results, the YOU icon displays.

LinkedIn also displays icons for people who have premium accounts, have Job Seeker accounts, or are OpenLink members. Refer to Chapter 6, "Communicating with Other LinkedIn Members," for a reminder of how LinkedIn classifies its members and how you can communicate with them.

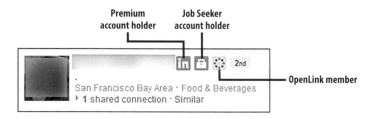

Interact with People on the Search Results Page

If you're already connected to a person, the Message button displays. You can click the Message button to send this person a message, or you can hover over the button to display a list of other options, including the following:

- **View Connections**—View this person's connections.

- **Share**—Share this person's profile with another LinkedIn member.

- **Find References**—Find other people on LinkedIn who might be able to provide a reference for this person. Requires a premium account.

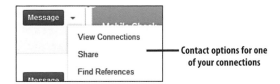

Contact options for one of your connections

If you aren't connected to a person, the Connect button displays. You can click the Connect button to send an invitation or hover over the button to display a list of other options, including the following:

- **Save**—Save this profile to the Saved tab on your Contacts page.

- **Get Introduced**—Request an introduction from someone you both know.

- **Send InMail**—Send an InMail to this person. You must have a premium account to send InMail unless this person is an OpenLink member.

- **Share**—Share this person's profile with another LinkedIn member.

- **Find References**—Find other people on LinkedIn who might be able to provide a reference for this person. Requires a premium account.

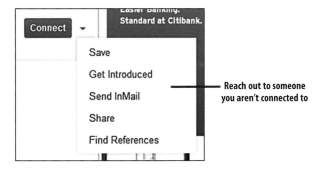

Reach out to someone you aren't connected to

Refer to Lesson 6 for more information about the available options for contacting others on LinkedIn.

Narrowing People Search Results

When you search for the name of a specific individual, the search results should display a short list (unless the individual has a common name). But what if you can't remember someone's last name or you're searching for LinkedIn members who meet general criteria, such as anyone with a PMP certification or anyone who has ever worked for IBM? In this case, your search might return hundreds or even thousands of results, exceeding the 100-result viewing limits associated with a personal account.

To narrow your search results, use one of the search filters on the left side of the search results page. Another option is to perform an advanced search that targets specific criteria. The search criteria are identical for both options.

Narrow your search results

Perform an Advanced People Search

If you want to search for very specific criteria, you can perform an advanced people search. An advanced search offers you the same options as the search filters on the search results page, but you can perform it all in one step on the Advanced People Search page.

1. Click the Advanced link on the navigation bar.

2. Enter your search criteria.

3. Click the Search button to display search results.

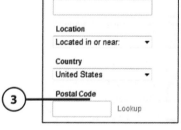

USING ADVANCED SEARCH TECHNIQUES

You can search on a variety of criteria using the Advanced People Search page or the search filters on the search results page, including the following:

- **Keywords**—Enter a keyword that LinkedIn searches for in member profiles. The best keywords are terms that don't fit any of the other search criteria and are specific words that a member might include on a profile. For example, entering a name or location wouldn't be appropriate here, but terms such as Java, PMP, WordPress, CPA, copywriting, Photoshop, PRSA, and so forth would work well.

- **First Name**—Enter the first name of the member you want to find.

- **Last Name**—Enter the last name of the member you want to find.

- **Title**—Enter a job title and specify any filters in the drop-down list. Options include Current or Past, Current, Past, or Past Not Current.

- **Company**—Enter a company name and specify any filters in the drop-down list. Options include Current or Past, Current, Past, or Past Not Current.

- **School**—Enter the name of a college or university.

- **Location**—Select a country, postal code, and distance range.

- **Relationship**—Filter search results based on people's position in your network: 1st degree connections, 2nd degree connections, fellow group members, and 3rd degree connections that are combined with everyone else on LinkedIn.

If you have a premium account, you can search by advanced criteria including Groups, Years of Experience, Function, Seniority Level, Interested In, Company Size, Fortune (Fortune 50 to Fortune 1000 firms), and When Joined.

Save a People Search

If you perform the same searches frequently, saving them can reduce redundant data entry.

Saved Search Limits

As a free basic account holder, you can save up to three searches and receive email updates either weekly or monthly. To save more searches, click the Upgrade Your Account link to sign up for a premium account. If you want to receive daily email updates on your saved searches, you must select the Executive account option.

1. Click the Save Search link on the search results page.

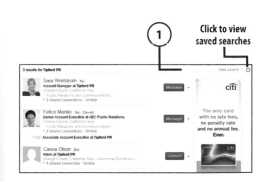

Click to view saved searches

2. Enter a search name for this search. LinkedIn displays your original search term by default.

3. Specify when you want to receive email updates of your search results: Weekly, Monthly, or Never.

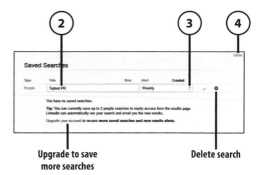

Upgrade to save more searches

Delete search

Saved Search Tips

You don't have to receive updates by email, but this can be a time-saver if you're interested in following updates to your saved search. For example, recruiters might want to know about new LinkedIn members who match specific search criteria. Or job seekers might want to know about new LinkedIn members who work at companies they're interested in working for.

4. Click the Close link to close the dialog box.

Integrate LinkedIn
with Outlook

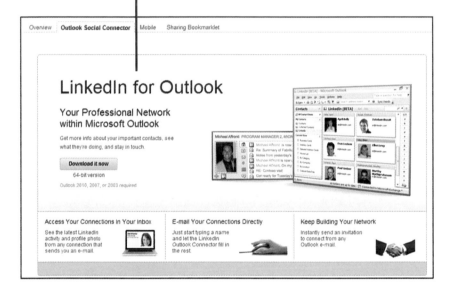

In this lesson, you explore tools that enable you to maximize your time on LinkedIn and integrate with other websites and software.

→ Exploring LinkedIn tools
→ Creating an email signature
→ Using the Sharing Bookmarklet
→ Using LinkedIn mobile apps

8

Using LinkedIn Tools

As a LinkedIn member, you want to maximize the value you receive from the site. Integrating the vast amount of data on LinkedIn with other applications such as browsers, popular websites, and email clients is one of the best ways to do that.

Exploring the LinkedIn Tools Page

The LinkedIn Tools page offers several tools, toolbars, and widgets that enhance your LinkedIn experience, both on and off the site. Options include

- **Outlook Social Connector**—Manage your LinkedIn network from Microsoft Outlook 2003, 2007, 2010, or 2013.

- **Email Signature**—Create a customized email signature from your profile data to use with popular email systems.

- **Mac Search Widget**—Search LinkedIn from your Mac Dashboard.

- **Google Toolbar Assistant**—Add a LinkedIn search button to the Google Toolbar in Internet Explorer.

- **Mobile**—Access your LinkedIn network via mobile devices, such as the iPhone, iPad, Android, BlackBerry, and Windows Phone.

- **Sharing Bookmarklet**—Share news articles, blog posts, and other interesting web content with LinkedIn members, including your connections and fellow members of groups.

LinkedIn Tools page

Click the Tools link on the bottom menu to open the LinkedIn Tools page.

Tools link

This chapter describes some of the most popular LinkedIn tools in more detail. You access all these tools from the LinkedIn Tools page.

Working with Email Signatures

LinkedIn enables you to create an email signature that includes links to your profile and other popular LinkedIn features. You can use your LinkedIn email signature with popular email systems such as Microsoft Outlook, Outlook Express, Mozilla Thunderbird, and Yahoo! Mail.

Create an Email Signature

1. Click the Try It Now button in the Email Signature section of the LinkedIn Tools page.

2. Select a layout for your email signature from the drop-down list.

3. A preview of your signature with the selected layout appears on the page.

4. Enter the contact information you want to appear on your signature in the Business Information, Contact Information, and Work Address sections.

5. If you want to include a company logo or your photo, enter the image's URL in the Image Selection field.

6. Select any or all of the following check boxes to place links on your email signature: "Professional Profile" link, "See Who We Know in Common" link, or "We're Hiring" link.

Image Tips

Your image must be in the GIF, JPG, or PNG format; no larger than 50KB; and no larger than 100×60 in size. Click the Show link to display your image. Be aware that the way you add an image can vary depending on the browser you're using.

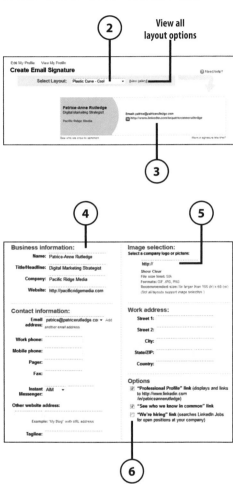

View all layout options

Use Your LinkedIn Profile Photo on Your Signature

To use your LinkedIn photo, right-click the photo on your profile and choose Copy Image Location or Copy Shortcut from the menu. (The menu option varies by browser.) Paste (Ctrl+V) this link in the Image Selection field.

7. Click the Click Here for Instructions link to save your signature.

8. In the pop-up box that opens, copy your signature code by clicking in the text box and pressing Ctrl+C on your keyboard.

9. Select your email client from the drop-down list. Instructions for using the email signature in your email system appear.

10. Click the Close This Window link to close the window and install your new email signature.

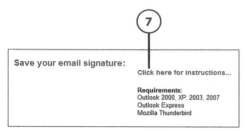

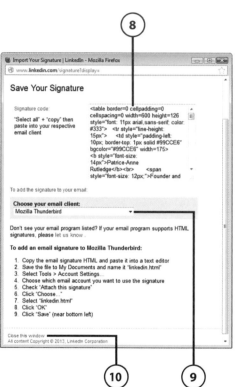

Using the Sharing Bookmarklet

LinkedIn offers a Sharing Bookmarklet that enables you to share content on LinkedIn from any of the following browsers: Internet Explorer, Firefox, Chrome, and Safari. Using the bookmarklet, you can easily share news stories, blog posts, and other interesting web content with LinkedIn members, including your connections and fellow members of groups.

It's Not All Good

AVOID TOO MUCH SHARING

Although this feature provides a convenient way to share content on LinkedIn, it's a powerful tool that you shouldn't overuse. To generate a positive response from other LinkedIn members, focus on sharing only the most useful, relevant content that affects the majority of group members. For example, share a top news story, an insightful report that affects your industry, or a content-rich post from your blog. Don't share promotional material or sales pages. Also avoid over-sharing of the same content, such as posting a blog link several times a day.

To install the bookmarklet, select the Sharing Bookmarklet tab on the LinkedIn Tools page and follow the onscreen instructions. The installation steps vary based on your browser. For example, Internet Explorer requires that you add the bookmarklet to your favorites menu, whereas Chrome, Safari, and Firefox ask that you simply drag the icon to your browser toolbar.

Sharing Bookmarklet for Chrome

Sharing Bookmarklet for Internet Explorer

Encouraging Others to Share Your Content

If you have your own website or blog and want to encourage others to share your content on LinkedIn, they can do so even if they don't use the Sharing Bookmarklet. See the section "Using LinkedIn Plugins" later in this chapter for more information about installing plugins on your site.

Share with the Bookmarklet

1. In your browser, navigate to the page you want to share.

2. Click the Share on LinkedIn button on the toolbar. On some browsers, this is called the Share in LinkedIn button.

3. Select the Share an Update check box to post this content as an update that displays on your profile and on your connections' home pages.

4. Select the Post to Groups check box to select a group you belong to. LinkedIn posts your content to the Discussions tab.

5. Select the Send to Individuals check box to send to one or more of your 1st degree connections.

6. Click the Share button to share this web page.

Enter your own comments about this content

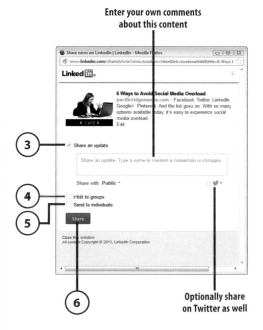

Optionally share on Twitter as well

Exploring LinkedIn Mobile Applications

LinkedIn offers four device-specific mobile apps you can access from the LinkedIn Mobile page:

- **LinkedIn for Phone**—A mobile app that's available for Android, iPhone, BlackBerry, and Windows phone devices

- **LinkedIn for iPad**—An app designed specifically for the iPad

- **Contacts**—A LinkedIn contacts app for the iPhone that includes job change and birthday alerts as well as relationship history

- **Pulse**—An app for the iPhone and Android that enables you to create a custom, shareable news feed

To access these apps from LinkedIn, click the Mobile link on the bottom menu or the Mobile tab on the LinkedIn Tools page.

LinkedIn Mobile page

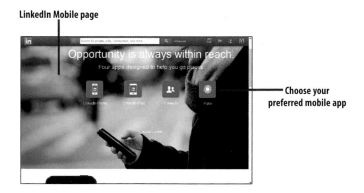

Choose your preferred mobile app

LinkedIn for Phone (Android version)

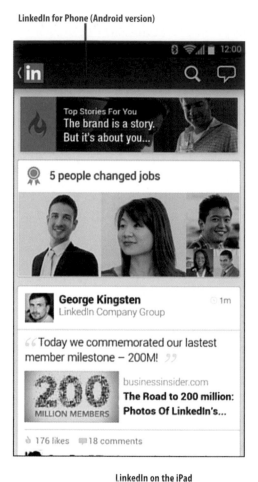

LinkedIn on the iPad

Access LinkedIn via the Mobile Web Link

If none of the mobile apps work for you, another option for accessing LinkedIn on the go is the mobile web link (m.linkedin.com). Type this link in your mobile browser to access a version of LinkedIn that's designed for mobile browsers.

It's Not All Good

LINKEDIN MOBILE APP LIMITATIONS

Be aware that although LinkedIn mobile apps are powerful tools, they don't include every feature available on the desktop version of LinkedIn. In addition, the features available vary by app.

Exploring Other LinkedIn Tools

Here's a quick roundup of even more tools and features that can enhance the time you spend on LinkedIn.

Use LinkedIn Plugins

LinkedIn offers numerous plugins you can use on your website to encourage interaction with LinkedIn. Sample plugins include Share on LinkedIn, Follow Company, and Member Profile. See https://developer.linkedin.com/plugins to learn more about the available plugins.

LinkedIn plugins

LinkedIn Plugins for WordPress Users

If you use WordPress, many social sharing plugins also enable site visitors to share your content on LinkedIn. Some examples include Flare (http://wordpress. org/plugins/flare) and AddThis (www.addthis.com). You can also add a LinkedIn profile badge to your sidebar with the FP LinkedIn Profile plugin (http:// wordpress.org/plugins/fp-linkedin-profile).

View LinkedIn Labs Tools

The LinkedIn Labs page (http://engineering.linkedin.com/linkedinlabs) offers several interesting tools for LinkedIn members looking to move beyond the basics.

Move beyond the basics with LinkedIn Labs tools ———

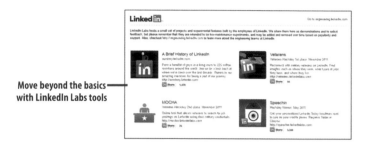

Some samples include

- **LinkedIn InMaps**—LinkedIn InMaps displays a visual map of your entire LinkedIn network. For your InMap to provide meaningful data, you must have at least 50 connections and at least 75% of your profile complete. If you meet these requirements, your InMap displays a color-coded representation of your LinkedIn network that you can zoom to view in more detail, label, and share with your network.

- **LinkedIn Swarm**—With Swarm, you can view a moving tag cloud of LinkedIn activity over the past hour. Swarm analyzes company and title searches, jobs posted, blog entries, and shared articles. In other words, it provides real-time insight into what's hot and trending.

- **Resume Builder**—Create a professionally designed resume based on your LinkedIn profile. You can choose from several resume formats and download a PDF of your resume.

- **Year In Review**—View everyone in your network who changed jobs in a specific year.

Create a polished resume from your
LinkedIn profile with Resume Builder

Influencer Posts tab

All Influencers tab   All Channels tab

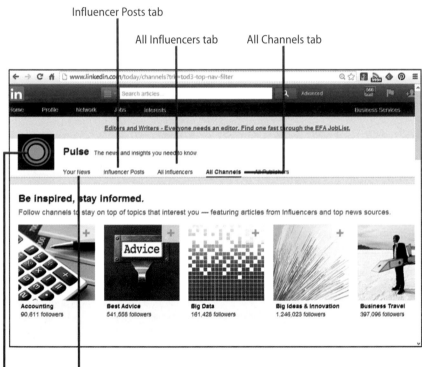

LinkedIn
Pulse
main page

Your News tab

In this chapter, you explore LinkedIn Pulse and discover how to customize your news and follow relevant influencers and channels.

Viewing News on LinkedIn Pulse

LinkedIn Pulse displays relevant professional news and insights directly on your home page. You can customize its content so that you view only information about your profession, industry, and interests rather than the general news you view on other sites. In addition, LinkedIn enables you to follow high-level industry leaders, called *influencers*, as well as specific channels related to your interests.

Viewing and Customizing News

LinkedIn displays four articles in the LinkedIn Pulse section at the top of your home page: a main feature with a large image and three additional articles. This content is recommended for you based on the influencers and channels you follow. If you aren't following any sources, LinkedIn offers news targeted to the industry you specified when you signed up for an account.

It's Not All Good

CAN I REMOVE LINKEDIN PULSE?

Although many people enjoy reading customized news when they log in to LinkedIn, others aren't so eager to do so. Unfortunately, you can't remove LinkedIn Pulse from your home page. You can, however, customize its content. In this chapter, you discover how to make LinkedIn Pulse more relevant to you.

View LinkedIn Pulse Content

On LinkedIn Pulse, you can view both influencer posts and news from leading news sources such as *The New York Times*, *The Wall Street Journal*, TechCrunch, Inc., Fox Business, and more.

1. If you aren't already on your home page, click the Home link.

2. Preview the current news on LinkedIn Pulse.

3. Click a title to open the article.

What Happens Next?

If you click a link that leads to an article on an external website, LinkedIn opens the article in another browser window. If you click a link that leads to an influencer post, LinkedIn opens the post within LinkedIn, where you can comment on and share it.

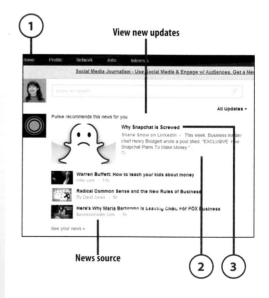

View new updates

News source

How Do I Comment on a News Article?

If you want to comment on a news article within LinkedIn rather than just go to the original article, you need to do so from the LinkedIn Pulse page. See the next section, "View More News."

View More News

To view more news as well as comment, share, and like news articles, you need to go to the LinkedIn Pulse page.

1. On the LinkedIn home page, click the LinkedIn Pulse link.

2. The Your News tab displays.

3. Click a title to open an article.

4. Click the Like icon to like this article.

5. Click the Comment icon to add a comment.

6. Click the Share icon to share with other LinkedIn members.

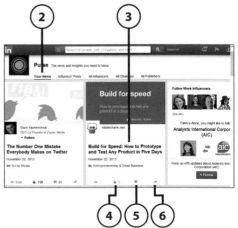

Its Not All Good

YOUR LINKEDIN PULSE ACTIVITY IS PUBLIC

Remember that commenting on or liking content on LinkedIn Pulse is a public action. Others can see your activities, and LinkedIn might display your photo. Before making a comment on or liking a controversial topic, consider whether you want your LinkedIn network to see this action.

Customize Your News

LinkedIn enables you to customize what displays in the LinkedIn Pulse section on your home page.

1. On the LinkedIn home page, pause over the All Updates drop-down list.

2. Specify the updates you want to see.

LinkedIn Pulse Mobile App

Optionally, you can also install the Pulse Mobile app if you want to read news on the go. See Chapter 8, "Using LinkedIn Tools," for more information on the Pulse app.

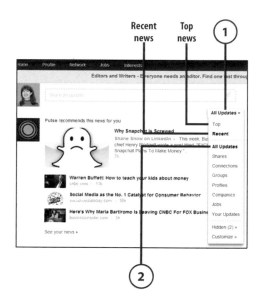

Customize LinkedIn Pulse Email Alerts

By default, LinkedIn sends you a weekly email update with the latest from LinkedIn Pulse. If you want to change your delivery frequency—or opt out of email updates entirely—you can do so on the Account

& Settings page. See Chapter 4, "Customizing Your LinkedIn Settings," to learn about additional email customization options.

1. Pause your mouse over your photo.

2. Click the Review link for Privacy & Settings.

3. Click the Communications tab.

4. Click the Set the Frequency of Emails link.

5. Click the Edit icon next to Updates and News.

6. Specify your preferred email frequency for LinkedIn Pulse updates: Daily Digest Email, When Influencers You're Following Post, Weekly Digest Email, or No Email.

7. Click the Save Changes button.

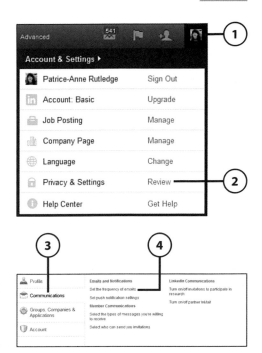

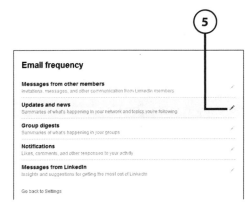

Exploring Influencers

Influencers are well-known industry leaders whom LinkedIn has invited to contribute original content to LinkedIn Pulse. Popular influencers include Virgin Group founder Richard Branson (who currently has the most followers by far), President Barack Obama, Bill Gates, UK Prime Minister David Cameron, Deepak Chopra, and many more.

Follow an Influencer

When you follow an influencer, this person's posts display in the LinkedIn Pulse section of your home page and on the Influencer Posts tab. The All Influencers tab provides a wide selection of interesting people to follow. LinkedIn identifies the influencers you currently follow with a check mark and those you don't follow with a plus sign.

1. On your home page, click the LinkedIn Pulse link.

Another Way to Find Influencers

Alternatively, select Pulse from the Interests menu and click the All Influencers tab to find influencers to follow.

Click the plus sign to follow

Click the check mark to unfollow

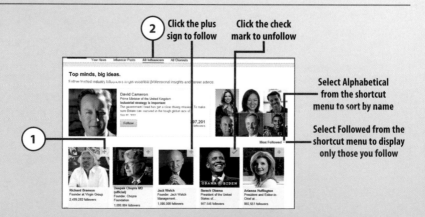

Select Alphabetical from the shortcut menu to sort by name

Select Followed from the shortcut menu to display only those you follow

2. Select the All Influencers tab.

3. Click the plus sign (+) on the image of an influencer to start following.

View an Influencer's Content

You can view all of an influencer's content on a single page. This is also a good way to pre-view what an influencer has to say before deciding whether or not to follow this person.

1. On the All Influencers tab, click the image (not the plus sign or check mark) of the influencer whose page you want to view.

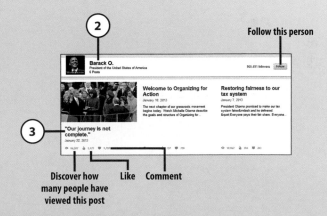

2. LinkedIn displays this person's page.

3. Click a post to open it.

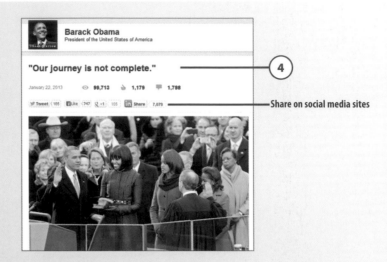

4. LinkedIn displays the post.

View Influencer Posts

LinkedIn displays selected influencer posts in the LinkedIn Pulse section on your home page, but you can also view all these posts in one place on the Influencer Posts tab on your LinkedIn Pulse page.

The Influencer Posts tab

Unfollow an Influencer

If you no longer want to follow an influencer, you can unfollow that person with a single click. To do so, go to the All Influencers tab and click the check mark on the image of the influencer you want to unfollow. After you unfollow someone, this person's posts no longer display in your LinkedIn Pulse content.

Click the check mark to unfollow

Exploring Channels

Channels are broad topics of interest to many LinkedIn members. They include content from relevant influencers as well as selected third-party news articles. Sample channels include Technology, Entrepreneurship & Small Business, Green Business, Healthcare, Marketing Strategies, Professional Women, Social Media, Higher Education, and more. LinkedIn displays content from the channels you follow in the LinkedIn Pulse section on your home page.

Follow a Channel

LinkedIn identifies the channels you currently follow with a check mark and those you don't follow with a plus sign.

1. On your home page, click the LinkedIn Pulse link.

2. Select the All Channels tab.

3. Click the plus sign (+) on the channel you want to follow.

>>>Go Further

PREVIEWING A CHANNEL

If you want to preview a channel before following it, click its image. LinkedIn displays that channel's page where you can read its content.

The Green Business channel

Interact with channel content

Unfollow a Channel

If you no longer want to follow a channel, you can unfollow it with a single click. To do so, navigate to the All Channels tab and click the check mark on the channel you want to unfollow. After you unfollow a channel, its posts no longer display in your LinkedIn Pulse content.

Click the check mark to unfollow

Follow Publishers on LinkedIn

You can also follow select publishers on LinkedIn, including *The Wall Street Journal*, *Time* Magazine, CNBC, USA TODAY, *Forbes*, and more. To view available publishers, click the All Publishers tab on the Pulse page.

Follow top publishers on LinkedIn

Search for jobs by keyword,
title, or company

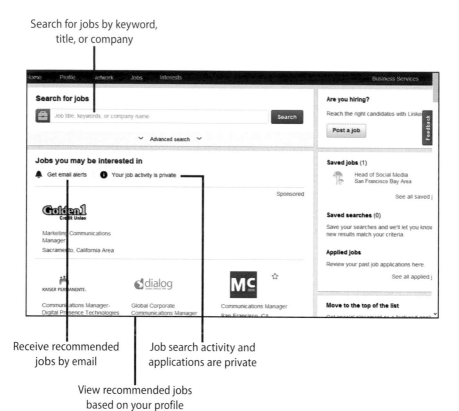

Receive recommended
jobs by email

Job search activity and
applications are private

View recommended jobs
based on your profile

In this chapter, you explore how to use LinkedIn as an effective job search tool, find and apply to job postings, and use LinkedIn's many other features for job seekers. Topics in this chapter include:

→ Attracting recruiters and hiring managers
→ Searching job postings
→ Viewing job postings
→ Performing an advanced job search
→ Applying for a job
→ Finding recruiters and hiring managers
→ Upgrading to a Job Seeker premium account

Finding a Job

LinkedIn offers many powerful tools for job seekers, including a comprehensive jobs database, profiles of thousands of recruiters and hiring managers, detailed company information, and much more.

Attracting Recruiters and Hiring Managers

LinkedIn is an excellent tool for job seekers, but you need to create a stellar profile and develop a solid network if you want to maximize your results. Here are eight tips for making the most of LinkedIn as a job search tool.

- **Complete your profile**—LinkedIn reports that members with a complete profile generate 40 times more opportunities than those whose profiles aren't complete.

LinkedIn displays your number of connections

- **Develop a solid network of connections**—Having a reasonable number of connections helps you make the most of LinkedIn's many features. Although connecting with anyone and everyone isn't a smart strategic move, having at least 100 relevant connections maximizes the benefits of using LinkedIn.

Demonstrate your expertise
with skills and endorsements

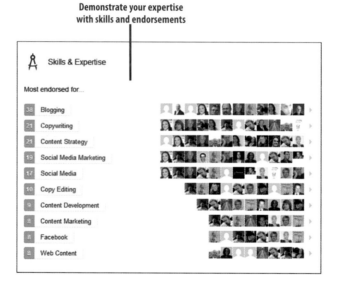

- **Add relevant skills to your profile**—Listing your key skills on your profile makes it easier for recruiters to find you and quickly identify your skillset. You can also have colleagues endorse you for these skills.

Solid recommendations enhance your profile

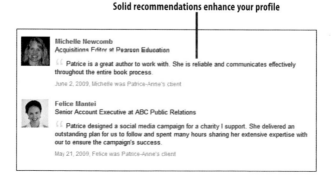

- **Get recommendations**—A complete profile includes at least three recommendations. Aim for recommendations from managers, executives, or actual clients. Peer recommendations, particularly those that you "trade" with colleagues by recommending each other, carry far less weight.

- **Include keywords that are relevant to your profession and industry**—These include specific skills, certifications, and degrees. Recruiters search for these words, and your profile should include them if you want to be found.

- **Focus on results, not a list of duties**—Remember that your profile is a concise summary of your qualifications, not a resume (although you can attach one if you like). Emphasize your results and accomplishments; don't just list tasks you performed.

- **Post a resume or portfolio**—Attach PDFs or other documents to your profile.

- **Indicate on your profile that you're seeking employment**—If you're unemployed, include this information in your status, professional headline, or summary. Don't sound desperate, but do let your network know that you're looking for opportunities.

See Chapter 2, "Creating Your LinkedIn Profile," and Chapter 11, "Working with LinkedIn Recommendations," for more information.

It's Not All Good

BEWARE DIGITAL DIRT

Keep in mind that many recruiters now search the Web for background information on potential candidates. Before starting your job search, review your online presence for any "digital dirt" and remove it if possible. For example, look for any photos, videos, or content that could compromise your professional reputation. Having outdated information or content with errors or misspellings can also negatively affect your image.

Don't just focus on your LinkedIn profile. Also review your other social media profiles and search for your name on Google and other popular search engines.

Searching for Jobs

A big advantage for job seekers is LinkedIn's large database of high-quality job postings.

Other Ways to Find Jobs

Although the Jobs page is LinkedIn's primary job search tool, you should also search the Jobs tab on any groups you belong to and the Careers tab on the company pages of your target employers. To do a quick search for jobs, use the search box on the top navigation menu.

Search Job Postings

The Jobs page makes it easy to search for the perfect job on LinkedIn.

1. Click the Jobs link.

View Recommended Jobs

Below the search box on the Jobs page, LinkedIn lists jobs you might be interested in based on the information you entered on your profile. For example, if you work in project management, you could view a list of jobs in this field.

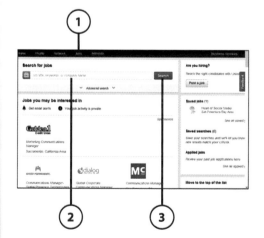

2. Enter keywords related to your job search in the Search for Jobs box. For example, you could enter a job title, a job skill, or the name of a target company.

3. Click the Search button to displays results on the Job Search Results page.

4. Click a job title to open a detailed job posting.

5. Sort jobs by relevance, your relationship to the job poster, or the date posted (most recent or earliest).

6. Click the Save Search link to save this job search and have results sent to you via email on a regular basis, such as daily, weekly, or monthly.

7. Click the Save Job button to save a specific job posting.

View Saved Jobs
You can view the jobs you save on the Saved Jobs section on the right side of the Jobs page.

8. Click the Similar link to view jobs similar to a specific job posting. LinkedIn displays jobs that are the most similar to the one you selected.

Refine Your Search Criteria
Refine your search criteria using the fields on the left side of the page. The fields in the Job Search box are nearly identical to the fields on the Advanced Search page. See the "Performing an Advanced Job Search" section later in this chapter for more information.

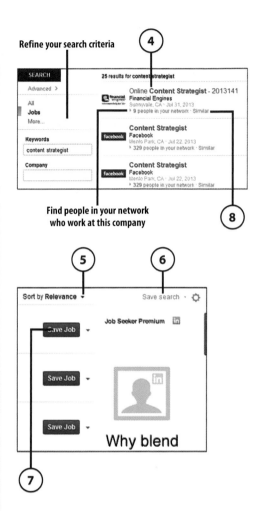

Refine your search criteria ④

Find people in your network who work at this company ⑧

⑤ ⑥

⑦

View Job Postings

The content listed on a job posting varies according to what the hiring company chooses to display. The content in a job posting's sidebar also varies according to what type of connection you have to the poster and the connections you have to people working at that company. A job posting might include some or all the following features:

View more details about this company

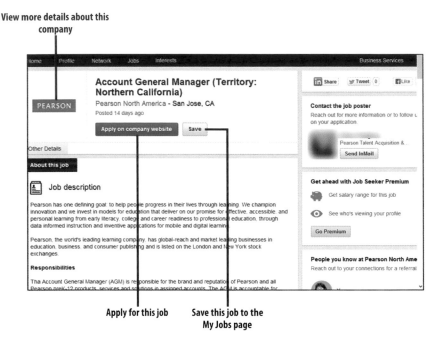

Apply for this job   Save this job to the My Jobs page

- A header listing the job title, location, and company name.

- The Share button.

- A button to apply for the job. The Apply Now button displays if you can apply for the job directly on LinkedIn. The Apply on Company Website button displays if a company prefers to use its own application process. See the "Applying for a Job" section later in this chapter for more information.

- Click the Save button. Click to save this job for future viewing on the My Jobs page.

- The About This Company section, which enables you to learn more about this company. Click the Follow Company link if you want to follow this company's activity on LinkedIn.

Learning more about this company

Follow this company on LinkedIn

- The Similar Jobs section, which lists jobs that are similar to the one you're viewing.

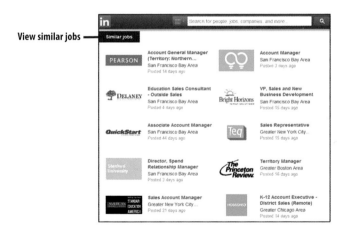

View similar jobs

- The Share Job button. Click to open the Share on LinkedIn dialog box, which enables you to send a message to a connection who might be interested in this job, share with fellow group members, or share on Facebook, Twitter, or with your LinkedIn network (displays with other network updates).

- The Tweet button. Click to share directly on Twitter.

- The Like button. Click to like this job on Facebook.

- The Contact the Job Poster box with a button to contact the job poster directly on LinkedIn. Depending on your connection to the job poster, a link to request an introduction or send InMail could appear. Refer to

Chapter 6, "Communicating with Other LinkedIn Members," for more information about LinkedIn introductions and InMail.

- The People You Know at [Company Name] box. Click one of the links in this box to display the LinkedIn members in your network who work at this company. These people could provide you inside information about potential job opportunities.

- The People Also Viewed box, which lists jobs that people who viewed this posting also viewed.

Perform an Advanced Job Search

If you want to search for jobs based on specific criteria, try an advanced job search.

1. Click the Jobs link.

2. Click the Advanced Search link.

3. Enter keywords (such as job title, company name, skill, or certification) in the Keywords text box. Refer to Chapter 7, "Searching on LinkedIn," for more information on using advanced search criteria.

4. Specify the criteria for your search. For example, you can narrow your search results by location, function, or industry.

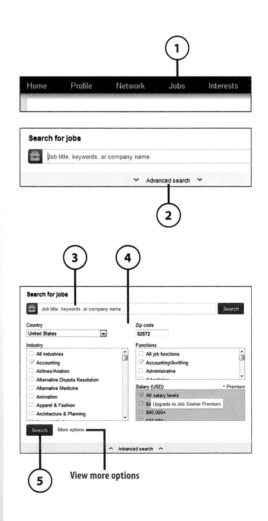

Specify Only the Most Important Criteria

You don't need to specify criteria in all the fields available on the Advanced Search page. Start with a few choices and then narrow or expand your search based on your search results.

5. Click the Search button.

6. LinkedIn displays matching job search results.

More Job Search Options

Click the More Options link to view more advanced search options such as date posted or experience level. If you have a Job Seeker premium account, you can search by salary. See the "Upgrade to a Job Seeker Premium Account" section later in this chapter for more information.

Applying for a Job

LinkedIn offers two ways to apply for jobs based on the way the company posting a job handles its recruitment. If the Apply on Company Website button displays on a job posting, clicking this button takes you to the company's external website where you can apply for the job. If the Apply Now button displays on the job posting, clicking this button directs you to a job application form on LinkedIn. This section shows you how to complete LinkedIn's own job application form.

Apply for a Job on LinkedIn

1. Click the Apply Now button.

Update Your Profile

LinkedIn includes your profile with your application. If you need to update this data before applying, click the Update Your Profile link to open the Edit Profile page. A detailed, error-free profile increases your chances of success.

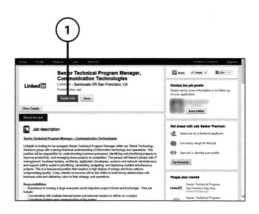

2. Enter a telephone number where the recruiter can reach you.

3. Click the Upload a File link to upload a resume or cover letter.

Cover Letter Tips

A good cover letter summarizes strengths and accomplishments that are relevant to the job and is personalized for the target job.

4. Click the Browse button to select a document from your computer.

Resume Formats

You can upload your resume as a Microsoft Word document or PDF of no more than 5MB. LinkedIn attaches your uploaded resume in its original format.

5. Select the Follow check box if you want to follow this company on LinkedIn.

6. Click the Submit button to submit your application.

Review Your Job Applications

To review the jobs you've applied for, return to the Jobs page and click the See All Applied Jobs link.

Finding Recruiters and Hiring Managers

The good news for job seekers: Thousands of recruiters and hiring managers maintain profiles on LinkedIn. Using the Advanced People Search page is a great way to find them.

ADVANCED SEARCH TECHNIQUES FOR JOB SEEKERS

Here are several ideas for finding the right recruiters and hiring mangers on LinkedIn's Advanced People Search page:

- To search by keyword, select Staffing and Recruiting in the Industry field and enter keywords related to the type of job you're looking for. If applicable, enter location criteria.

- To search for recruiters by company, enter Recruiter in the Title field and the name of a company you want to work for.

- To search for recruiters by location, enter Recruiter in the Title field plus relevant location information.

- To search for hiring managers by company, enter the name of a company you want to work for and select Hiring Managers from the Interested In drop-down list (requires a premium account).

Search for People Who Can Hire You

Use the Advanced People Search page to find the people you want to contact.

1. Select People in the quick search box.

2. Click the Advanced link.

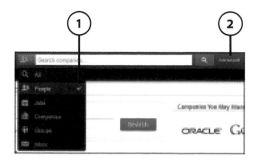

3. Select your search criteria.

4. Click the Search button.

Try Different Search Options

Searching for appropriate contacts is a combination of art and science, so you might need to revise your search criteria several times before you find the appropriate people.

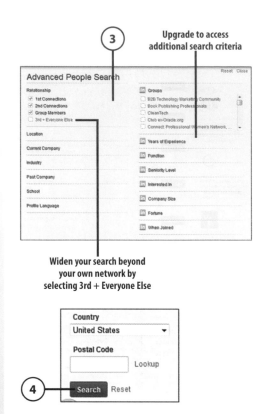

Upgrade to access additional search criteria

Widen your search beyond your own network by selecting 3rd + Everyone Else

It's Not All Good

DON'T SPAM RECRUITERS AND HIRING MANAGERS

Remember that LinkedIn is a networking and research tool, not a means of spamming prospective recruiters and employers. When you find good targets for your job search, review their profiles carefully to determine the best way to contact them. Some recruiters provide links to external sites for job candidates.

Alternatively, consider sending a brief message to hiring managers who indicate they are open to job inquiries.

Exploring Job Seeker Premium Accounts

LinkedIn offers many free features and opportunities for job seekers. If you need access to LinkedIn premium features to aid in your job search, however, consider upgrading to a Job Seeker premium account.

>>>Go Further

EXPLORING JOB SEEKER PREMIUM ACCOUNTS

Job Seeker accounts offer extra features to help you in your job search. With a premium account, you can

- Access a list of people who viewed your profile

- Position yourself as a featured applicant, moving your applications to the top of a recruiter's list

- Display a Job Seeker badge on your profile

- View detailed salary data for LinkedIn job postings

- Access job search advice and training

The Job Seeker account comes with 5 InMail messages per month; the Job Seeker Plus account comes with 10 InMails per month. Job Seeker Basic account holders don't have access to InMail.

Upgrade to a Job Seeker Premium Account

1. Click the Upgrade link.

2. Click the For Job Seekers tab.

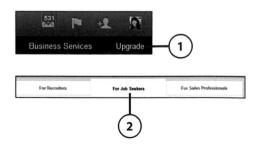

3. Select the Annual option to pay up front for a full year.

4. Select the Monthly option to be billed for your premium each month.

Get a Discount

If you sign up for an annual plan, you receive a substantial discount—up to 25% per year. Before choosing this option, however, it's a good idea to test a premium account for a month to verify it's the right option for you.

5. Review what's included in each plan in the Compare Plans section. For example, the higher priced plans include more InMail messages, introductions, searches, and so forth.

6. Click the Start Now button below your preferred plan.

7. Enter your payment information including credit card details and your address.

8. Click the Review Order button to verify and finalize your purchase.

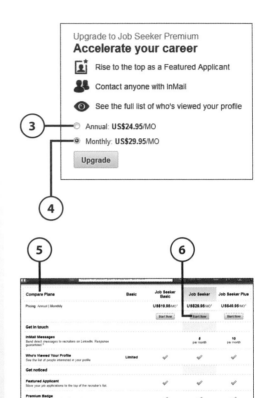

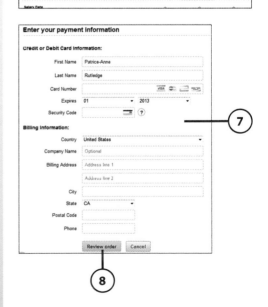

The Recommendations section on your profile

Recommendations you've received

Recommendations you've given

Recommendations

Received (1) ▾   **Given (3)**

Felice Mantei
Associate Account Executive

❝ Felice worked for me for two years at Tipford PR. She's an excellent writer with solid social media and media relations skills who also a polished and poised presenter. I would welcome the opportunity to work with Felice again.

August 31, 2013, Sara managed Felice at Tipford PR

Annie Richards

❝ Annie is our "go to" copywriter for any content that requires a strong grasp of the latest technologies. In particular, she has extensive knowledge of mobile and green technology and can convey this expertise in a way that excites and motivates customers. She's always on time and on target and is a delight to work with.

September 13, 2010, Sara was Annie's client

In this chapter, you discover how to request, provide, manage, and revise professional recommendations on LinkedIn.

→ Requesting a recommendation
→ Responding to a recommendation request
→ Accepting recommendations
→ Hiding recommendations you've given or received
→ Requesting a revised recommendation
→ Editing or withdrawing a recommendation

Working with LinkedIn Recommendations

LinkedIn enables you to request recommendations from and provide recommendations to the people in your professional network. Recommendations are a powerful networking tool, so consider carefully whom you want to ask for a recommendation and whom you want to recommend as part of your overall LinkedIn strategy.

Understanding LinkedIn Recommendations

LinkedIn offers four types of recommendations:

- **Colleague**—You worked with this person at the same company as a manager, peer, or employee.

- **Business Partner**—You worked with this person in another capacity; he or she was not a colleague. For example, you worked at partner companies, you performed volunteer or association work together, this person was a client, and so forth.

- **Student**—You were a teacher, advisor, or fellow student at the same school.

- **Service Provider**—You hired this person to perform services.

Recommendations Versus Endorsements

A *recommendation* is written text that describes a LinkedIn member's performance and qualifications for a specific position. An *endorsement* is a stamp of approval for a 1st degree connection's qualifications for a single skill. No written text is involved; you can endorse a skill with a single click. See Chapter 12, "Working with LinkedIn Endorsements," for more information.

>>>Go Further

EXPLORING THE LINKEDIN RECOMMENDATION PROCESS

The recommendation process involves several steps between two people to ensure both approve the recommendation before it is final. For example, if Oliver wants to request a recommendation from his former manager, Sophie—a common type of request—the process requires four steps:

- **Step 1**—Oliver sends a recommendation request to Sophie.

- **Step 2**—Sophie receives the request and submits a recommendation for Oliver.

- **Step 3**—Oliver receives a notification about Sophie's recommendation and accepts the recommendation.

- **Step 4**—LinkedIn displays the recommendation on Oliver's profile.

Obviously, this process assumes that both Oliver and Sophie approve each step. LinkedIn also offers options for you to request clarifications and changes. If you write an unsolicited recommendation for a connection without receiving a recommendation request, your process starts at step 2 with submitting the recommendation.

Requesting Recommendations

Receiving recommendations from managers, colleagues, and clients can help you achieve your networking goals on LinkedIn. LinkedIn suggests that a complete profile should include at least three recommendations for maximum effectiveness.

Before you send your requests, however, think about what you want to achieve. Be clear about your goals so your connections write recommendations that help you achieve them. For example, if you want to move into a management position, you should request a recommendation that discusses your leadership abilities. If you want to change careers, emphasize crossover skills.

Let Your Connections Know You Want a Recommendation

Although LinkedIn notifies your connections when you request a recommendation, it's a good idea that this message doesn't come as a surprise. Talk to the people you want to recommend you so they're aware of your request and know what to emphasize in their recommendations.

It's Not All Good

DON'T MASS PRODUCE RECOMMENDATION REQUESTS

Although you can request a recommendation from up to 200 connections at a time, it's a much better practice to personalize each recommendation request you send. If you really want to send your request to more than one person, however, click the View All Connections button to select your recipients.

Request a Recommendation

You can request a recommendation from one of your connections from the Edit Profile page.

1. Select Edit Profile from the Profile menu.

2. Scroll down to the Recommendations section and click the Edit icon.

3. Click the Ask to Be Recommended link.

4. Select the job or school related to your recommendation request.

Keep Your Profile Up to Date

The drop-down list displays only positions and schools you've already entered on your profile. If you haven't done this, click the Add a Job or School link to complete this step first.

---

5. Start typing the name of the connection you want to ask for a recommendation. Select the correct name from the drop-down list of options that appear.

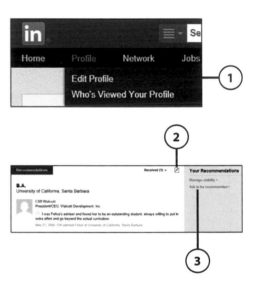

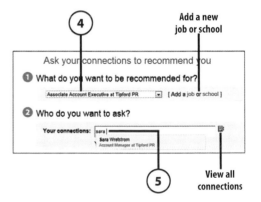

Add a new job or school

View all connections

6. Create your message asking for a recommendation.

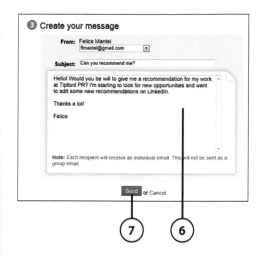

❸ Create your message

From: Felice Mantei
flmantei@gmail.com

Subject: Can you recommend me?

Hello! Would you be will to give me a recommendation for my work at Tipford PR? I'm starting to look for new opportunities and want to add some new recommendations on LinkedIn.

Thanks a lot!

Felice

Note: Each recipient will receive an individual email. This will not be sent as a group email.

Send or Cancel

7   6

Customize Your Request

LinkedIn provides sample message text for you, but you should customize this for each request. Be specific, and let your connection know what you want to achieve with this recommendation. You don't need to add a salutation; LinkedIn does this automatically.

7. Click the Send button.

What Happens Next?

LinkedIn sends your recommendation request to its target recipient. If you selected more than one person, each person receives an individual message. See the section "Responding to Recommendation Requests," next to learn what happens when a connection receives your recommendation request.

Responding to Recommendation Requests

LinkedIn sends a message to your inbox when you receive recommendation requests. The default subject line for these messages is "Can You Recommend Me?" unless the person requesting the recommendation modified this text.

Depending on the type of recommendation you want to provide (colleague, business partner, service provider, or student), the exact steps required to create a recommendation differ. This section explains how to create each type of recommendation. Although LinkedIn identifies student requests automatically, you need to decide whether you want to provide a colleague, business partner, or service provider recommendation when you receive a standard request.

Finding Recommendation Requests

If you don't respond to recommendation requests right away, you can find them by filtering your inbox messages for recommendations. Refer to Chapter 6, "Communicating with Other LinkedIn Members," for more information about working with your inbox.

Personalizing Recommendations

LinkedIn offers sample recommendation text, but you need to replace this with your own recommendation. Write a concise, specific recommendation that relates to the position and the goals of the person you're recommending. In addition, you can add a personal message to the person you're recommending in the Personalize This Message box. This text doesn't appear on the recommendation itself.

It's Not All Good

CONSIDER CAREFULLY WHO YOU RECOMMEND

Consider carefully before recommending someone on LinkedIn. Remember that your reputation is based not only on who recommends you, but also on who you recommend. Is this someone you would recommend in the real world? If not, reply privately to the person explaining that you don't feel comfortable giving the recommendation. For example, you might not know the person well enough for a recommendation, or your experience working together might not have been a positive one.

Respond to a Recommendation Request for a Colleague or Business Partner

If the person requesting a recommendation is a colleague or a business partner, follow these steps.

1. Pause over the inbox icon on the LinkedIn toolbar.

2. Click the message title. Unless your connection changed this, it should read, "Can You Recommend Me?"

3. Click the Write Recommendation button in the message detail.

4. Specify whether this recommendation is for a colleague or a business partner.

5. Click the Continue button.

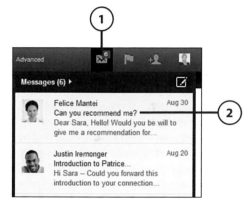

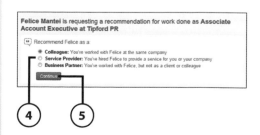

6. Specify your working relationship with this person.

7. Enter your title at the time.

8. Write your recommendation in the Written Recommendation box.

9. Click the View/Edit link.

10. Enter a personalized message to the person you're recommending.

11. Click the Send button to send the recommendation and accompanying message.

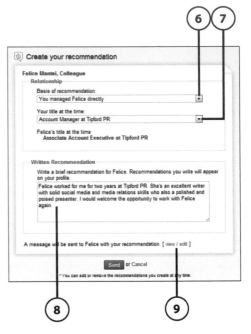

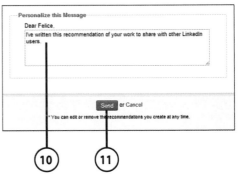

Respond to a Recommendation Request for a Service Provider

If the person requesting a recommendation is a service provider, follow these steps.

1. Pause over the inbox icon on the LinkedIn toolbar.

2. Click the message title. Unless your connection changed this, it should read, "Can You Recommend Me?"

3. Click the Write Recommendation button in the message detail.

4. Select the Service Provider option button.

5. Click the Continue button.

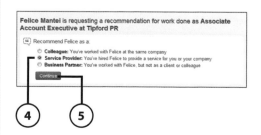

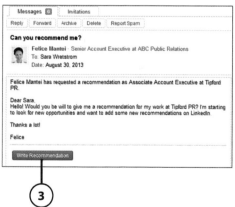

6. Select a service category.

7. Select the year you first hired this person.

8. Select this service provider's three top attributes.

9. Write your recommendation in the Written Recommendation box.

10. Click the View/Edit link.

11. Enter a personalized message to the person you're recommending.

12. Click the Send button to send the recommendation and accompanying message.

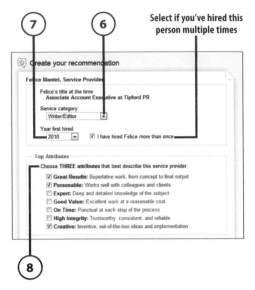

Select if you've hired this person multiple times

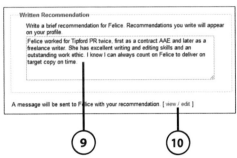

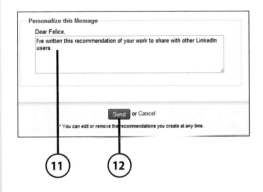

Respond to a Recommendation Request for a Student

If the person requesting a recommendation is a student, follow these steps.

1. Pause over the inbox icon on the LinkedIn toolbar.

2. Click the message title. Unless your connection changed this, it should read, "Can You Recommend Me?"

3. Click the Write Recommendation button in the message detail.

4. Indicate how you know this person.

5. Select your title at the time.

6. Write your recommendation in the Written Recommendation box.

7. Click the View/Edit link.

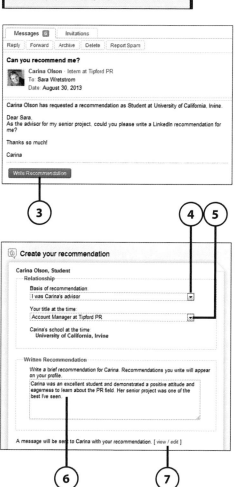

8. Enter a personalized message to the person you're recommending.

9. Click the Send button to send the recommendation and accompanying message.

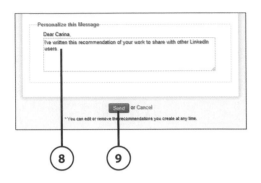

MAKING AN UNSOLICITED RECOMMENDATION

At times, you might want to recommend your connections even if they don't send you a recommendation request. Go to the profile of the person you want to recommend, scroll down to the Recommendations section, and click the Recommend [First Name] link. From here, follow the instructions in the "Responding to Recommendation Requests" section earlier in this chapter to write a recommendation for a colleague, business partner, service provider, or student.

You can recommend your connections even if they don't request it

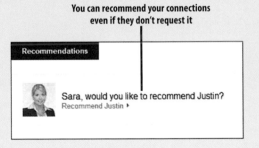

Managing Recommendations You've Received

The first step in handling a recommendation you've received is to decide whether or not to accept it. LinkedIn also puts you in control of whether to display or hide specific recommendations and enables you to request recommendation revisions.

REVIEW YOUR RECOMMENDATIONS ON A REGULAR BASIS

Several times a year, you should review your recommendations to verify that they're still relevant to your current goals. You might want to hide a recommendation that's no longer relevant or request updated recommendations from those who have recommended you in the past.

Accept Recommendations

When someone recommends you, LinkedIn sends a notification message to your inbox. If you indicate you want to receive email notifications on the Account & Settings page, LinkedIn also notifies you by email.

Finding Recommendation Requests

If you don't respond to recommendation requests right away, you can find them later by filtering your inbox messages for recommendations. Refer to Chapter 6 for more information about working with your inbox.

1. Pause over the inbox icon on the LinkedIn toolbar.

2. Click the message title.

3. Review the recommendation.

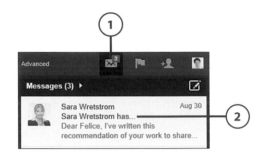

Hiding a Recommendation

By default, LinkedIn displays new recommendations on your profile. Optionally, you can select the Hide This Recommendation on My Profile option button if you want to hide a recommendation. In general, displaying your recommendations is a good promotional tool. One common reason for selecting this option is to hide unsolicited recommendations you don't want others to view.

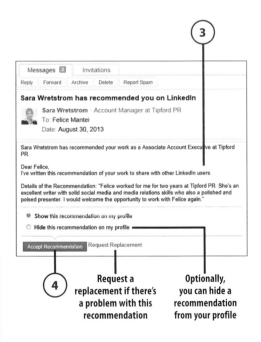

4. Click the Accept Recommendation button. LinkedIn displays it on your profile below its related position or school as well as in the Recommendations section.

Requesting a Replacement

Click the Request Replacement link to ask for a revised recommendation. This option is useful if the recommendation isn't accurate, contains misspellings, or doesn't focus on your current goals or accomplishments. To ensure that you receive a more appropriate recommendation, be sure to specify *why* you need a replacement.

Request a replacement if there's a problem with this recommendation

Optionally, you can hide a recommendation from your profile

Hide Recommendations You've Received

By default, LinkedIn displays the recommendations you've received below each related position as well as on the Received tab of your profile's Recommendation section. Optionally, you can hide any or all of these recommendations.

1. On the Edit Profile page, scroll down to the Recommendations section and click the Edit icon.

2. Click the Manage Visibility link.

3. Click the Manage link next to the position that contains the recommendations you want to hide.

4. Remove the check mark next to the person whose recommendation you want to hide.

5. Click the Save Changes button.

Restoring Recommendations

If you later decide you do want to display a hidden recommendation, replace the check mark next to the people whose recommendations you want to restore.

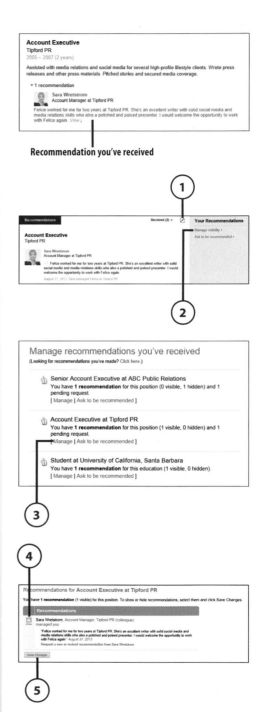

Recommendation you've received

Request a Revised Recommendation

LinkedIn enables you to request a revised recommendation from someone who has recommended you. Be sure to communicate clearly what you're looking for in your revised recommendation. For example, you might want to revise an older recommendation if your job duties for the same position have changed or you want to emphasize a different aspect of your job for future career growth.

1. On the Edit Profile page, scroll down to the Recommendations section and click the Edit icon.

2. Click the Manage Visibility link.

3. Click the Manage link next to the position that contains the recommendation for which you want a revision.

4. Click the Request a New or Revised Recommendation from [Name] link.

5. Explain your reason for requesting a revision.

6. Click the Send button.

When to Request a New Recommendation

If you receive a promotion or have a new job title, it's better to add a new position and request a new recommendation for that job rather than revising an existing recommendation.

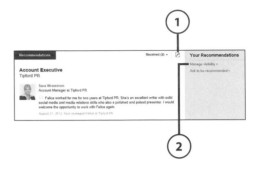

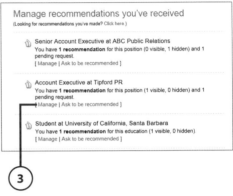

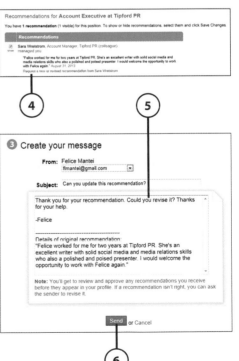

Managing Recommendations You've Given

After you've given recommendations, LinkedIn enables you to edit or withdraw them at any time. You can also control which recommendations display on your profile.

Edit a Recommendation You've Given

1. On the Edit Profile page, scroll down to the Recommendations section and click the Edit icon.

2. Click the Manage Visibility link.

3. Click the Given tab.

4. Click the Edit link next to the person whose recommendation you want to edit.

5. Modify your recommendation.

6. Click the Send button.

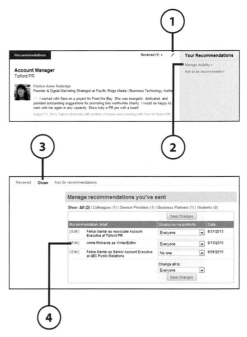

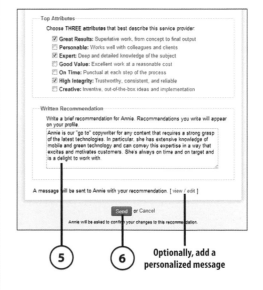

Optionally, add a personalized message

Withdraw a Recommendation You've Given

If you no longer want to recommend someone, you can permanently delete your recommendation.

1. On the Edit Profile page, scroll down to the Recommendations section and click the Edit icon.

2. Click the Manage Visibility link.

3. Click the Given tab.

4. Click the Edit link next to the person whose recommendation you want to edit.

5. Click the Withdraw This Recommendation link.

6. Click the Confirm button.

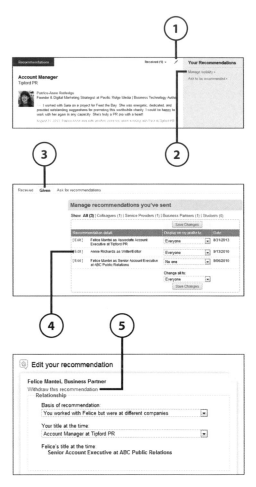

Hide Recommendations You've Given

By default, LinkedIn displays the recommendations you've given on the Given tab of your profile's Recommendation section. Optionally, you can hide any or all of these recommendations.

1. On the Edit Profile page, scroll down to the Recommendations section and click the Edit icon.

2. Click the Manage Visibility link.

3. Click the Given tab.

4. Select No One from the drop-down list next to the person whose recommendation you want to hide.

Displaying to Connections Only

Another option is to display recommendations you've given only to your connections rather than to everyone on LinkedIn.

5. Click the Save Changes button.

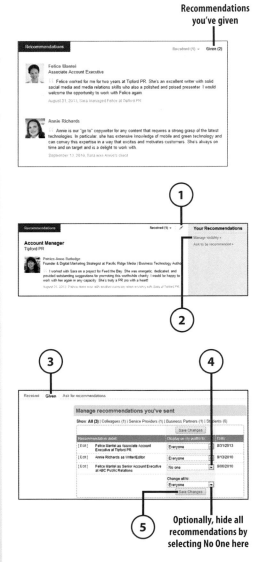

Recommendations you've given

Optionally, hide all recommendations by selecting No One here

Number of endorsements for this skill

Click the blue + to remove your endorsement

Photos of the connections who endorsed you

View a complete list of endorsers for this skill

Click the gray + to endorse

View skills outside the top 10

In this chapter, you explore how to give and receive endorsements on LinkedIn. Topics include:

→ Endorsing skills
→ Removing an endorsement
→ Viewing endorsement notifications
→ Hiding a single endorsement
→ Hiding all endorsements
→ Adding skills
→ Deleting skills

Working with LinkedIn Endorsements

LinkedIn enables you to endorse the skills of your 1st degree connections with a single click—and they can endorse your skills just as easily. Even though an endorsement isn't as detailed as a recommendation, it does offer an easy way to provide social proof of the skills the people in your network possess.

Your 10 skills with the most endorsements display in the Skills & Expertise section of your profile, along with photos of the 12 most recent connections who endorsed each skill.

Giving Endorsements

Endorsing the skills of your connections is a simple task—you can do so in a matter of seconds. Remember to give endorsements judiciously, however. Just because it's easy to endorse skills doesn't mean you should endorse hundreds of skills at once. Focus on endorsing people you actually know for their strongest skills.

Endorsements Versus Recommendations

An endorsement is a stamp of approval for a 1st degree connection's qualifications for a single skill. No written text is involved; you can endorse a skill with a single click. A recommendation is written text that describes a LinkedIn member's performance and qualifications for a specific position. See Chapter 11, "Working with LinkedIn Recommendations," for more information.

Endorse Skills at the Top of a Profile

At the top of a connection's profile, LinkedIn prompts you to endorse this person's skills.

1. Click the x next to any skill you don't want to endorse.

2. Optionally, type another skill you want to endorse.

3. Click the Endorse button.

4. Your photo displays next to the endorsed skills in the Skills & Expertise section (scroll down to view this section).

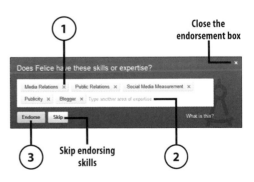

Close the endorsement box

Skip endorsing skills

Endorse Skills in a Profile's Skills & Expertise Section

You can also endorse your connections' skills in the Skills & Expertise section of their profiles.

1. Scroll down to the Skills & Expertise section on a connection's profile.

2. Click the gray + (plus sign) to endorse a skill.

3. Your photo displays next to the skill and the + turns blue.

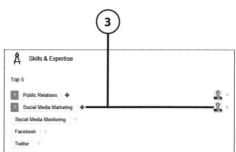

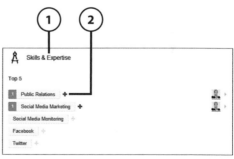

Remove an Endorsement

If you endorsed a skill by mistake or no longer want to endorse someone for any reason, you can remove an endorsement.

1. Scroll down to the Skills & Expertise section on a connection's profile.

2. Click the blue + (plus sign) to remove the endorsement for that skill. The sign changes to a – (minus) when you pause over it.

3. LinkedIn removes your photo next to the skill.

Receiving and Managing Endorsements

In addition to endorsing your connections for their skills, they can endorse your skills.

>>>Go Further

GETTING YOUR FIRST ENDORSEMENTS

Here are three steps to getting started with endorsements:

1. List your relevant skills—up to 50 skills in all—in the Skills & Expertise section of your profile. For a reminder on how to add skills, see Chapter 2, "Creating Your LinkedIn Profile."

2. Endorse the skills of your connections. This should prompt many people to return the favor and endorse you for skills they know you have. Be aware that you should use restraint in this step. In other words, don't endorse every connection you have for every skill they have listed. Instead, focus on selecting a handful of connections whose work you know well, and endorse them for several of their best skills.

3. Send a message to targeted connections letting them know that you've added new skills to your profile and would appreciate their endorsement. Like Step 2, this is most effective if you use it sparingly. Don't send an email to your LinkedIn network. Just focus on a handful of people who know your skillset and would be most likely to endorse you.

Using this approach, you should start seeing an increase in endorsements. After you add skills, your endorsements also grow naturally because LinkedIn prompts your connections to endorse these skills in several places throughout the site.

View Endorsement Notifications

When one of your connections endorses you for a skill, LinkedIn does the following:

- Sends you an email if you selected to receive notifications on the Communications tab of the Account & Settings page. See Chapter 4, "Customizing Your LinkedIn Settings," for more information.

- Notifies you about the endorsement in the activity list that displays when you click the flag icon at the top of your home page.

Click the flag icon to view recent endorsements

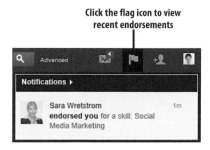

- Displays the endorsement in a blue box at the top of your profile if a connection endorsed you for a skill you didn't list in the Skills & Expertise section of your profile. You can add this skill to your profile or skip it.

New endorsed skill   **Remove the skill**

Add skill to your profile   **Skip adding skills to your profile**

- Displays the endorsement on your home page.

Your home page lists recent endorsements

- Displays the photo of the connection who endorsed you next to the endorsed skill in the Skills & Expertise section of your profile.

Hide an Endorsement

If someone endorses you for a skill and you don't want to display that person's endorsement on your profile, you can hide it on the Edit Profile page. (As a reminder, select Edit Profile from the Profile menu to open this page.) LinkedIn temporarily removes the selected person's photo from the Skills & Expertise section, yet retains all your other endorsements.

1. Click the Edit icon in the Skills & Expertise section.

2. Click the Manage Endorsements link.

3. Select the skill where you want to hide the endorsement.

4. Remove the check mark to the left of the person whose endorsement you want to hide.

Restoring an Endorsement

You can restore a hidden endorsement at any time by reselecting the check box next to an endorser's photo.

5. Click the Save button.

6. Scroll to the top of your profile and click the Done Editing button.

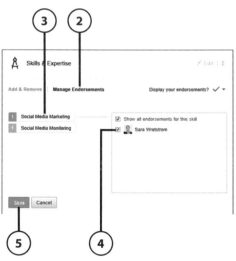

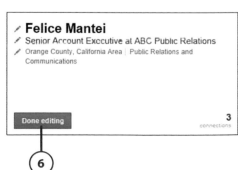

Hide All Endorsements

By default, LinkedIn displays your endorsements on your profile, which is the setting most people prefer. Optionally, you can hide all endorsements in the Skills & Expertise section on the Edit Profile page.

1. Click the Edit icon in the Skills & Expertise section.

2. Click the down arrow and select No, Do Not Show My Endorsements.

3. Click the Save button.

4. Scroll to the top of your profile and click the Done Editing button.

5. LinkedIn displays your skills, but not the photos of the people who endorsed you or the number of endorsements for each skill.

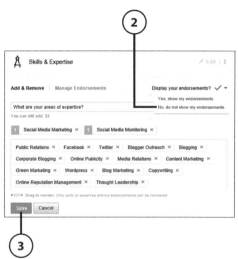

Displaying Endorsements

If you decide you want to display endorsements again, edit the Skills & Expertise section, click the down arrow, select Yes, Show My Endorsements, and click the Save button.

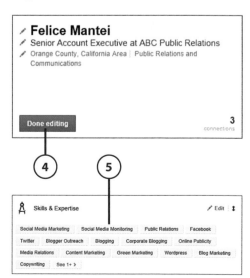

Add Skills

You can easily add more skills on your Edit Profile page—up to a total of 50.

1. Click the Edit icon in the Skills & Expertise section.

2. Start typing the skill you want to add. LinkedIn displays a list of potential matches you can choose.

3. Click the Add button.

4. Click the Save button.

5. Scroll to the top of your profile and click the Done Editing button.

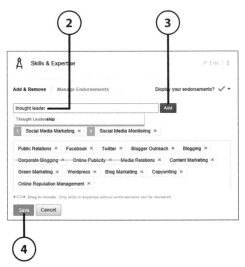

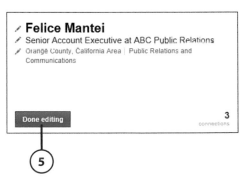

Delete Skills

If you no longer want to display a skill on your profile, you can delete it on the Edit Profile page. This is most common if you already have 50 skills and want to add a new skill or you change your career direction and no longer want to promote specific skills.

1. Click the Edit icon in the Skills & Expertise section.

2. Click the x to the right of a skill you want to delete.

3. Click the Save button.

4. Scroll to the top of your profile and click the Done Editing button.

Restoring a Deleted Skill

If you reinstate a previously deleted skill, LinkedIn attempts to find previous endorsements and display them.

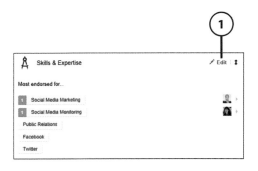

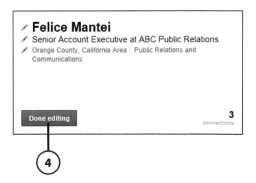

View job posting
slide show

Post a
job

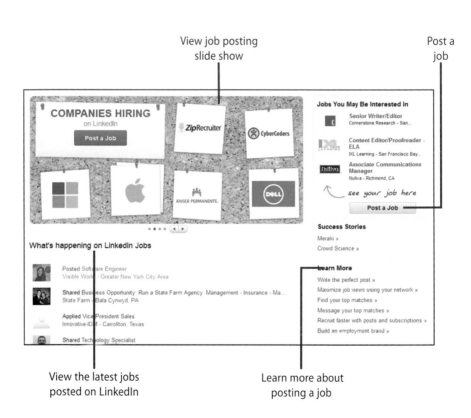

View the latest jobs
posted on LinkedIn

Learn more about
posting a job

In this chapter, you explore LinkedIn's options for recruiting top talent, including the following tasks:

→ Posting a job

→ Managing job postings

→ Posting a job on a group's Jobs tab

→ Searching for job candidates

→ Using LinkedIn Talent Solutions

Recruiting Job Candidates

Even in an employer's market, it can be difficult to find the right candidate, particularly for a job that requires specific expertise and experience. Fortunately, LinkedIn offers numerous options for recruiters, hiring managers, and small business owners to locate and recruit top talent.

On LinkedIn, you can

- Pay to post a 30-day job listing that's searchable by LinkedIn's millions of members (the exact price varies based on geographic location)

- Purchase job credits for discounted job postings

- Post a job on a group's Jobs tab

- Search for candidates using LinkedIn's advanced search features

- Perform reference searches on potential candidates

- Upgrade to a premium account to send more InMails to potential candidates

- Sign up for LinkedIn Talent Solutions, a comprehensive set of recruitment tools for larger companies

The option that's right for you depends on your budget, the size of your company, and the type of candidates you want to attract.

Posting Jobs on LinkedIn

Posting a job on LinkedIn provides a low-cost way to reach a targeted group of professionals, including both active and passive job seekers. LinkedIn charges a fixed fee for a 30-day job posting, which varies based on geographic location. If you plan to post multiple jobs, you can save money by purchasing discount job credits. If you're short on funds, posting to the Jobs tab on a related group is a free alternative.

Post a Job

LinkedIn offers a simple job posting form that enables you to post a job in minutes.

1. Select Post a Job from the Business Services drop-down menu.

2. Click the Post a Job button.

3. By default, LinkedIn displays the company name, description, and industry from your profile and the Company Page of your current company. Optionally, you can enter another company name, description, and industry.

4. Enter a job title and select basic position information such as experience level, job function, and employment type from the drop-down lists.

5. Enter a detailed job description of up to 25,000 characters.

Include Strategic Keywords

Candidates often search for jobs using keywords. Be sure your post contains the right keywords to attract top candidates. Job skills, certifications, and degrees—such as Java, copywriting, marketing, PMP, CPA, and MBA—are good keywords.

6. Describe the desired skills and experience for this position. You can enter up to 4,000 characters.

Formatting Job Descriptions

You can format the Job Description and Detailed Skills and Experience sections using the toolbar buttons to apply bold, italic, underlining, bulleted lists, and numbered lists.

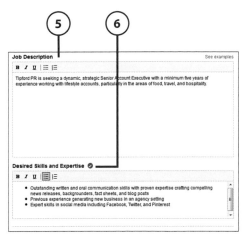

Sharing a Job on the Veterans Job Bank

If you want to attract veterans to your posting, select the check box in the Veterans Job Bank section. This shares your post at no additional charge on the NRD. gov's Veterans Job Bank website (www.nrd.gov/home/veterans_job_bank).

7. Specify how you want to receive applications. Your options include collecting applications on LinkedIn and receiving notification by email or directing applicants to an external website such as your company's own job listing page.

8. Indicate whether you want to display your profile on the job listing.

9. Specify the country and postal code for this job.

10. Specify whether you want to purchase a 30-day posting or a 5- or 10-job pack.

11. Click the Continue button.

Pricing Varies by Location

LinkedIn displays pricing information based on location and the number of jobs purchased. For example, a single job in a major metropolitan area such as San Francisco or New York costs $395. The same posting in a smaller market such as Indianapolis or Orlando costs $195.

Optionally, post your job on the Veterans Job Bank

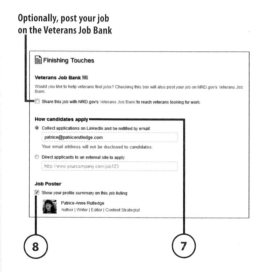

Save as a draft

Preview your job posting

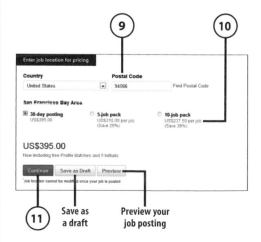

Saved Search Tips

Optionally, you can save your in-progress job posting to review later by clicking the Save as Draft button. To return to your saved draft, go to www.linkedin.com/job/consumer/manageConsumer while logged into LinkedIn.

Proofread Your Posting Carefully

Before posting your job, check it carefully for spelling, grammar, and content errors. Optionally, you can create your posting in Microsoft Word (or another word-processing application), run spell-check, and then copy to LinkedIn.

12. Click the Yes, Sponsor My Job check box to showcase your job posting on LinkedIn and specify your cost per click and budget.

13. Click the Continue button.

Sponsored Jobs

Sponsored jobs display at the top of the targeted job recommendations that each LinkedIn member sees. Each time someone clicks your job posting, you pay an amount you specify. You can also control the total budget for your sponsored job. By default, LinkedIn suggests a cost per click (CPC) of $1.75 and a total budget of $200, but you can adjust these amounts. The minimum CPC is $1.00, and the minimum total budget is $50.

(12)

Showcase your job to the right candidates

Even when they're not searching

- Feature your job atop targeted recommendations across LinkedIn and via email
- Target your ideal audience automatically
- You set the budget and only pay when someone clicks on your sponsored placement

☑ **Yes, sponsor my job**

Cost per click (only on sponsored placements)

1.75   USD

Total budget

200.00   USD

[Continue] [Go Back]

(13) **Return to previous page**

Sample sponsored job

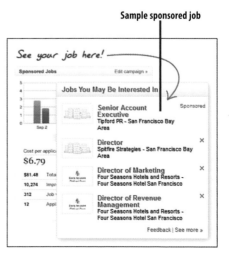

14. Enter your billing information and credit card data (unless you have available job credits—see the "Purchasing Job Credits" sidebar for more information).

15. Click the Review Order button to review and finalize your job posting.

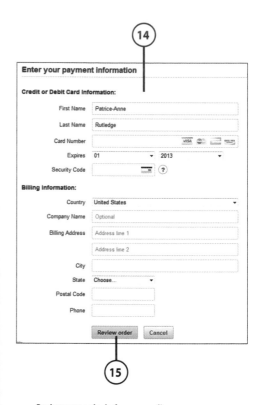

Review your order before proceeding

>>>Go Further

PURCHASING JOB CREDITS

Purchasing job credits can save you money if you post jobs on LinkedIn frequently, yet don't want to upgrade to LinkedIn Talent Solutions. (Talent Solutions is covered in the "Using LinkedIn Talent Solutions" section later in this chapter.) A job credit is a prepaid credit for posting a single job. Job credits come in packages of 5 or 10 credits with discounts off the standard fee for a single, full-price job posting.

Be aware, however, that if you purchase job credits for a lower-priced location, you can't use one of those credits to purchase a job posting for a higher-priced location. For example, you can't purchase job credits for Tulsa, Oklahoma (normally priced at $195 per job), and use them for a job posting in San Francisco, where job postings are $395 each.

Manage Job Postings

After you post a job—or save it as a draft—you can manage it on the Job Management page.

1. While logged into LinkedIn, navigate to www.linkedin.com/job/consumer/manageConsumer.

2. From the drop-down menu, specify whether you want to view draft jobs, active jobs, or closed jobs.

3. Click the Post link to post a draft job.

4. Click the Delete link to delete a draft job.

5. Click the Post a Job button to post another job.

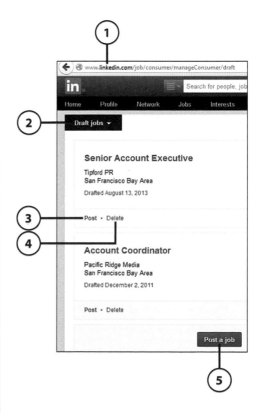

6. Click the Buy Credits button to purchase more jobs credits.

7. Click the Purchase History link to view your past job posting purchases.

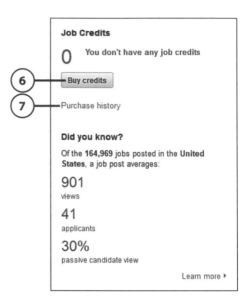

Job Credits

0 You don't have any job credits

6 —— Buy credits

7 —— Purchase history

Did you know?

Of the **164,969** jobs posted in the **United States**, a job post averages:

901
views

41
applicants

30%
passive candidate view

Learn more ›

Post a Job on a Group's Jobs Tab

A group's Jobs tab offers a free way to let targeted LinkedIn members know about open positions, but it doesn't offer the reach of a paid job posting. You must belong to a group to post on its Jobs tab. See Chapter 14, "Participating in LinkedIn Groups," for more information about joining groups. You can also share paid job ads on a group's Jobs tab.

It's Not All Good

DON'T POST JOBS ON THE DISCUSSIONS TAB

Be aware that most groups have rules about not posting jobs on the regular Discussions tab. Although you add a job using the share box on the Discussions tab, you must select the Job discussion type. This displays it on the Jobs tab where it belongs. If you post a job in the wrong place, the group owner could move it or another member could flag it.

1. Select Groups from the Interests drop-down menu.

2. Select your target group.

3. Enter a job title.

4. Enter additional job details.

5. Select Job as the Discussion Type.

6. Click the Share button.

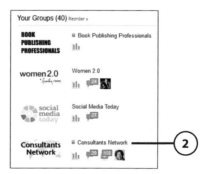

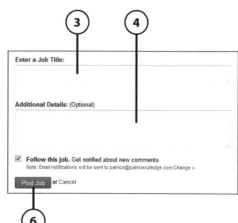

Searching for Job Candidates

At times, you might want to search for passive job candidates in addition to considering the candidates who apply directly for your open positions. Here are some search strategies for finding qualified passive candidates:

- View the people connecting to your connections who perform a similar job.

- Perform an advanced search for LinkedIn members who meet specific criteria. See Chapter 7, "Searching on LinkedIn," for more information.

Looking for candidates who meet targeted criteria —

- Search relevant groups for members who match your criteria. See Chapter 14 for more information.

PERFORMING REFERENCE SEARCHES

LinkedIn reference searches are a premium feature that let you search for LinkedIn members who worked at the same company at the same time as a candidate you're considering for a job.

Here are several ways to access the reference search feature:

- On the people search results page, click the down arrow to the right of the Message button or Connect button and select Find References.

- On the profile of someone who isn't your connection, click the down arrow to the right of the Send InMail button and select Find References.

- On the profile of someone who is your connection, click the down arrow to the right of the Suggest Connections button and select Find References.

LinkedIn offers two other ways to search for similar reference information at no cost. You can

- Click the name of a company on a candidate's profile and view the list of employees on the Company Page.

- Perform an advanced people search, specifying the candidate's company and location. Refer to Chapter 7 for more information on advanced searches.

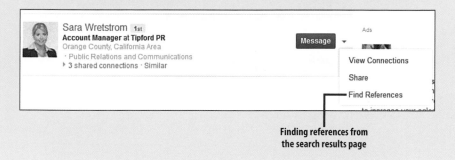

**Finding references from
the search results page**

Upgrade to Contact More Candidates

If you plan to contact potential job or reference candidates by InMail, consider upgrading to a premium account that includes a specified number of InMails per month. For more information, click the Upgrade link on the navigation menu.

Using LinkedIn Talent Solutions

LinkedIn Talent Solutions offers a comprehensive set of paid recruitment tools for major companies, including the following components:

- **LinkedIn Recruiter**—Enable a team of recruiters to collaborate, manage the recruitment process, source passive job candidates, and share multiple InMails per month

- **Jobs Network**—Post jobs with precision targeting, candidate match recommendation, and viral distribution

- **Career Pages**—Publish a Career Page for your company with custom content, including employee spotlights and video

- **Work with Us**—Place job ads on your employees' LinkedIn profiles

To learn more, click the Talent Solutions link on the bottom navigation menu.

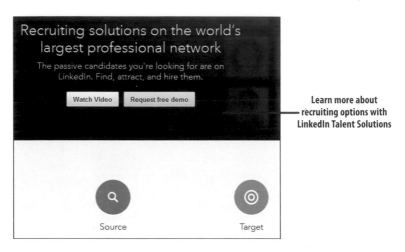

Learn more about recruiting options with LinkedIn Talent Solutions

A selection of
LinkedIn groups

See what's new in your groups

**BOOK
PUBLISHING
PROFESSIONALS**

**Book Publishing
Professionals** 🔒
26 Discussions
4 Jobs

women 2.0

Women 2.0
9 Discussions

social
media
today

Social Media Today
21 Discussions

**Consultants
Network**

Consultants Network 🔒
37 Discussions
31 Jobs

Technology Section
PRSA

PRSA Technology Section 🔒
1 Job

Club **ex-Oracle**

Club ex-Oracle.org 🔒
1 Discussion

*ORACLE
Alumni*

ORCL (Oracle) Alumni 🔒

UCIRVINE
ALUMNI

UCI Alumni 🔒

Web 2.0

Web 2.0
2 Discussions

Green Communicators

Informed Ideas For Writers 🔒

People
People

PeoplePeople 🔒

In this chapter, you find out how to participate in LinkedIn groups, manage the groups you join, and create your own group.

→ Searching for and joining groups
→ Participating in group discussions
→ Starting a discussion
→ Creating a poll
→ Using the Jobs tab
→ Using the Promotions tab
→ Managing your groups
→ Creating a group

14

Participating in LinkedIn Groups

LinkedIn groups offer a way for like-minded individuals to share and discuss relevant topics related to the focus of the group. With LinkedIn groups, you can network and share ideas with industry peers, discover job leads and recruit quality talent, promote your career or business, and learn about a wide range of professional topics.

Getting Started with LinkedIn Groups

LinkedIn groups take many forms. There are groups for alumni, associations, nonprofit organizations, professional interests, corporations, general networking, conference attendees, and personal interests.

>>>*Go Further*

OPEN GROUPS VERSUS MEMBERS-ONLY GROUPS

LinkedIn offers two types of groups: open and members-only. An open group allows all LinkedIn users to view its Discussions tab as well as comment on and like its posts. You must join, however, to start your own discussions. Open groups are also indexed by search engines and allow people to share group content on Facebook and Twitter. A members-only group requires approval of the group owner to join, and its content is private and can't be shared outside LinkedIn.

If you want to join a members-only group, be sure to verify whether there are any requirements for membership. Some groups, for example, require you to be an alumnus of a school or company or a paid member of a professional association.

It's Not All Good

LINKEDIN LIMITS THE NUMBER OF GROUPS YOU CAN JOIN

LinkedIn imposes a limit of 50 group memberships per account holder. If you reach 50 groups and want to join another, you need to leave a group of which you're currently a member. Because of this limit, it's important to consider carefully which groups will provide you with the most value and help you meet your goals.

Join a Group

You can search for groups to join from the search box at the top of any LinkedIn page.

Let LinkedIn Suggest Groups for You

Another way to find good groups to join is to let LinkedIn suggest groups for you. You can view recommended groups in the Groups You May Be Interested In section on the Your Groups page. (Select Groups from the Interests menu.)

1. Select Groups from the search menu.

2. Enter keywords related to the group you want to find. For example, you could enter the name of a company, school, professional association, skill, or interest.

3. Click the Search button.

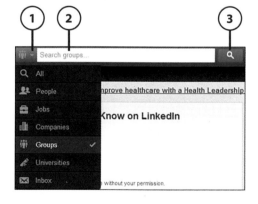

Options in the Drop-Down List

Before clicking the Search button, review the options that display in the drop-down list. If you're searching for a specific group by name, you might find it here and can click that group in the list to open it. If you're looking for all potential groups on a particular topic, clicking the Search button offers more choices.

4. LinkedIn displays potential matches.

View the best matches in the drop-down list

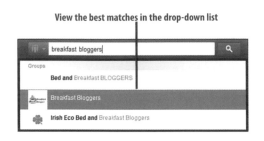

Keeping Your Group Activity Private

LinkedIn publishes an update to your network when you join a group with notifications enabled. If you don't want to let your network know when you join a new group, you can keep this activity private. For more information, see the section "Turn Off Group Notifications," in Chapter 4, "Customizing Your LinkedIn Settings." Also remember to hide this group's logo on your home page (see the section "Manage Group Settings," later in this chapter).

5. Click the View button to preview an open group.

6. Click the Join button to request to join a members-only group.

What Happens Next?

If you click the View button, you can preview the group and click the Join button in that group if you decide to join. You are given immediate access to the group and can modify your group settings. See the section "Manage Group Settings," later in this chapter.

If you click the Join button, LinkedIn sends the group owner your request. See the section "Follow Up on a Request to Join a Members-Only Group," next.

Lock icon indicates members-only group

View group statistics

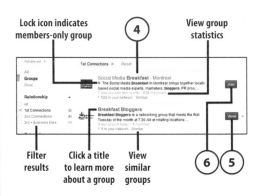

Filter results — Click a title to learn more about a group — View similar groups

Join this group

Click the Here link to manage group settings

Follow Up on a Request to Join a Members-Only Group

You can't participate in a members-only group until the group owner approves your membership. While you're waiting for approval, you can follow up with the group owner (give this person at least a week to respond before sending a follow-up request) or withdraw your request to join. If you clicked the Join button by mistake, withdrawing is the easiest way to resolve the problem.

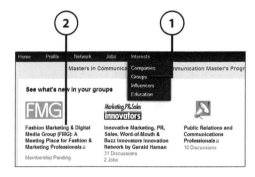

1. Select Groups from the Interests menu.

2. Click the title of the group whose membership is pending.

3. Click the Send Message to the Group Manager link to follow up on your request to join.

4. Click the Withdraw Request to Join link to withdraw your join request.

Participating in Group Discussions

Participating in discussions is one of the greatest values of joining a group. With LinkedIn group discussions, you can view discussion threads for relevant professional information, add a comment to a current discussion, start your own discussion, or share news and links with group members.

Focus on Quality, Professional Discussions

As with everything else on LinkedIn, focus on intelligent, meaningful discussions that add value to a group. Don't post a sales pitch or irrelevant comment just to lead people to your profile.

View Group Discussions

1. Select Groups from the Interests menu.

2. Click the title of the group you want to open.

3. Click the title of the discussion you want to open.

4. View the discussion's detail page.

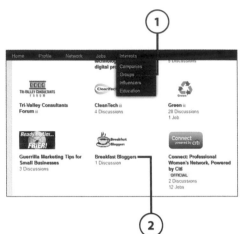

Group owner's recommended content

Pause over a poster's photo to learn more

View popular discussions

View recent discussions

Like a Discussion

If you find a discussion item particularly useful and interesting, you can show your support by clicking the Like link below it. This link is available on the Discussions tab or on a discussion's detail page. Liking a discussion alerts other group members as well as your followers that you found the discussion worthwhile. If you change your mind or click this link by mistake, you can unlike the discussion by clicking the Unlike link (the Like and Unlike links act as toggles). If others have previously liked a discussion, LinkedIn displays this number in parentheses after the Like link.

Like a discussion

Adding a Comment to a Discussion

You can add a comment to a discussion on the Discussions tab or on that discussion's detail page.

1. Start typing in the Add a Comment box below the post you want to comment on.

Where's the Add a Comment Box?

If no one has commented on or liked a post, this box doesn't display. Instead, click the Comment link to open the Add a Comment box.

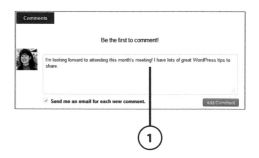

2. If you want to receive email notification of any new comments in this discussion, select the Send Me an Email for Each New Comment check box.

3. Click the Add Comment button to post your comment.

Editing or Deleting a Comment

After you post a comment, LinkedIn gives you 15 minutes to revise it. Click the Edit Comment link below your comment to make any changes. Click the Delete link to remove your comment from the discussion at any time.

4. LinkedIn displays your comment below the discussion.

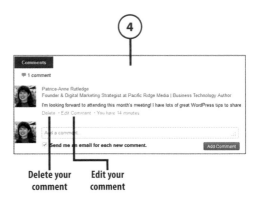

Delete your comment   Edit your comment

Share a Discussion

Sharing discussions on LinkedIn—or on other social sites such as Facebook, Twitter, or Google+—is a good way to gain visibility for open groups. The exact steps to share vary based on the site you're sharing on, but the concept is the same. In this example, you share a LinkedIn group discussion on your public LinkedIn news feed.

1. Click the Share link below an open discussion.

2. Click your preferred share button: LinkedIn, Twitter, Facebook, or Google+. In this example, you share on LinkedIn.

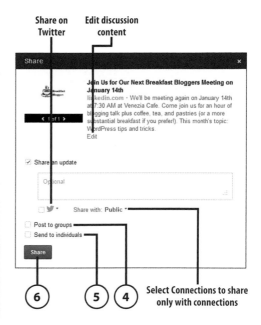

Share on Twitter

Edit discussion content

Where's the Share Link?
The Share link displays only on a discussion's detail page. It doesn't display below the discussion summaries on the Discussions tab.

3. Enter your comments about this discussion.

4. Optionally, post this discussion in another group.

5. Optionally, share this discussion in a message to one or more LinkedIn connections.

6. Click the Share button.

Select Connections to share only with connections

Follow Group Discussions and Members

If you want to know when someone adds a new comment to a discussion you find particularly relevant, you can follow the discussion. To do so, click the discussion title and click the Follow link on the detail page.

Follow this person

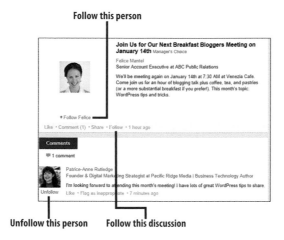

Unfollow this person   Follow this discussion

LinkedIn sends you an email anytime someone adds a comment. By default, you follow any discussion you start or comment on unless you specify that you don't want to receive email notification. If you decide you no longer want to follow a discussion, click the Unfollow link below it. (Unfollow displays only for discussions you're following.)

To follow a group member, click the Follow [First Name] link below that person's photo. You can unfollow people by clicking the Unfollow link below their name or by going to the Discussions You're Following page. (Click the Search tab to access this page.)

Reply Privately to a Discussion

If you don't want to add a public comment to a discussion, you can send its author a private message using one of the following options:

- On the Discussions tab, click the down arrow to the right of the discussion title and select Reply Privately from the menu, or...

Reply privately from the Discussions tab

- ...on a discussion's detail page, click the Reply Privately link below the discussion text.

Reply privately on a discussion's detail page

Flag Discussions and Comments

If you find a discussion or comment you feel is inappropriate, you can notify the group owner about it.

- You can flag a discussion as inappropriate (or belonging on the Jobs tab or Promotions tab) by clicking the down arrow to the right of its title on either the Discussions tab or discussion detail page and selecting the appropriate option from the menu.

- To flag a comment, click the Flag as Inappropriate link below it.

Flag a discussion

Flag a comment

Start a Discussion

On the Discussions tab, you can start your own discussion or share relevant links with other group members.

1. Enter up to 200 characters in the Start a Discussion box at the top of the Discussions tab. This text serves as your discussion headline, so consider carefully what you want to enter.

2. The section expands to include a second text box where you can add more details (up to 4,000 characters).

3. Specify a discussion type: General, Job, or Promotion.

4. Click the Share button.

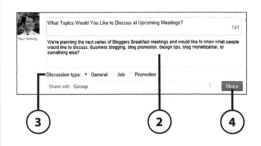

Inserting a Link in a Group Discussion

Optionally, you can insert a link in a group discussion by copying and pasting the URL in the Add More Details text box. LinkedIn searches for this URL and displays a title, description, and photo from the content it finds on this page. Click the title or description to edit.

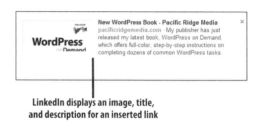

LinkedIn displays an image, title, and description for an inserted link

General, Job, or Promotion?

Selecting General displays your post on the Discussions tab, which is the default setting. Selecting Job displays a job posting on the Jobs tab. Selecting Promotion displays a post on the Promotions tab, which is reserved for sales pitches and other promotional content.

5

5.   LinkedIn displays your discussion on the Discussions tab.

Deleting Your Discussion

You can delete a discussion you posted by clicking the down arrow to the right of its title and selecting Delete from the menu.

It's Not All Good

DON'T OVERDO SELF-PROMOTION

Submitting your own articles, blog posts, or media coverage is acceptable, but don't overdo sharing only your own content. Submit only the most informative, meaningful content that offers value to the members of your group. If your content is sales-oriented, post it on the Promotions tab.

Create a Poll

A group's Polls feature enables you to poll group members about relevant professional topics and participate in polls other members create. A *poll* is a short question with the option of providing as many as five answers. Group members select their preferred answers, and the poll tallies the results. Be aware that this is an optional group feature. If you don't see the Polls icon on the Discussions tab, the group owner didn't activate polls.

1. Click the Poll icon on the Discussions tab.

2. Enter a question of up to 200 characters in the Ask a Question box.

Poll Character Limits

Poll questions can contain no more than 200 characters, and answers can contain no more than 40 characters. LinkedIn displays the number of characters remaining at the right side of each field. If you go over this limit, a negative number displays, and you need to revise your text. In addition, you can't include actual numbers or symbols in a poll, only text.

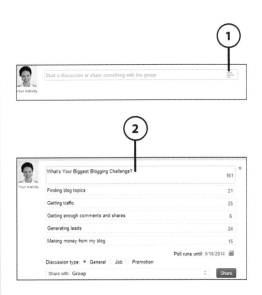

3. Enter your first potential answer of up to 40 characters in the Specify Up to 5 Answer Choices box.

4. Continue adding potential answers, up to a total of five.

5. Click the Share button to post your poll.

6. LinkedIn displays your poll.

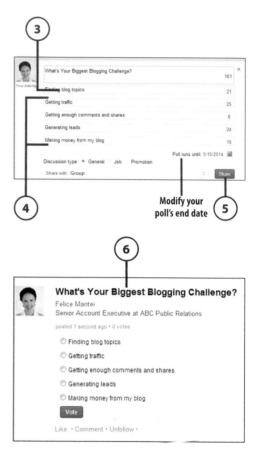

Modify your poll's end date ⑤

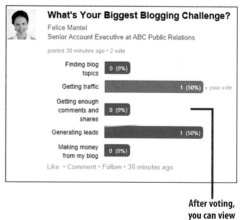

After voting, you can view poll results

Viewing Group Promotions

If the group owner has enabled this feature, a group includes a Promotions tab where members can post promotional content that isn't appropriate for the general Discussions tab. For example, you should post information about paid products and services, sales, and other promotions on this tab.

To post on the Promotions tab, create a discussion on the Discussions tab and select Promotion as the discussion type. See the section "Start a Discussion," earlier in this chapter.

Promotions tab

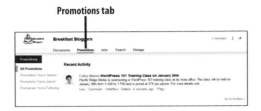

Viewing Group Job Postings

A group's Jobs tab enables you to view and search LinkedIn job postings shared by other group members as well as post job-related discussion items. This is also an optional group feature; the group owner can choose whether or not to include a Jobs tab.

To post a job on this tab, create a discussion on the Discussions tab and select Job as the discussion type. See the section "Start a Discussion," earlier in this chapter.

View Jobs on the Jobs Tab

Although the LinkedIn Jobs page offers more jobs for you to peruse, a group's Jobs tab can offer more targeted jobs.

1. Click a group's Jobs tab.

2. Sort jobs by relevance or date.

3. Filter jobs if the Jobs tab contains numerous postings.

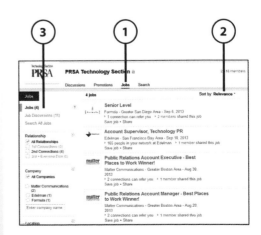

4. Click a title to view the detailed job posting with details on how to apply.

5. Click the Save Job link to save an interesting job.

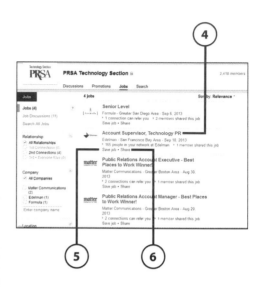

Viewing Your Saved Jobs

You can view the jobs you save on the Jobs page. (Click the Jobs link on the main LinkedIn menu.)

6. Click the Share link to share this job with other LinkedIn members or on Twitter or Facebook.

Other LinkedIn Job Tools

See Chapter 10, "Finding a Job," and Chapter 13, "Recruiting Job Candidates," to learn about more ways to find jobs and recruit candidates on LinkedIn.

Managing Your Groups

LinkedIn offers a lot of flexibility in how you participate in, manage, and view the groups you join. You can also search for and share specific group information and leave a group anytime you want.

View Your Groups

You can view a list of the groups you belong to by selecting Groups from the Interests menu.

Establishing Group Order

On the Account & Settings page, you can specify the order of the groups that display on the Your Groups page. See the section "Specify Group Display Order," in Chapter 4 for more information.

Select to display your groups

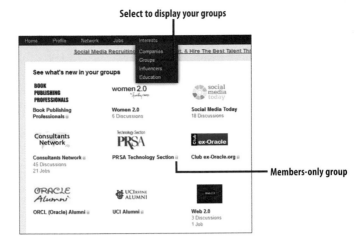

Members-only group

A lock icon displays to the right of any group that is members-only. If this icon doesn't display, the group is an open group.

To go to a group's Discussions tab, click the title of the group.

View Your Group Information on Your Profile

You can also view a list of the groups you belong to on your profile.

Groups section on a profile

View Basic Group Information

To view basic information about a group, click the *i* icon on the group page. This enables you to learn more about a group's goals as well as its owner, members, rules, and statistics. If you haven't joined an open group yet, reviewing this information is a good way to determine if the group is right for you.

View group information and setting

View group statistics

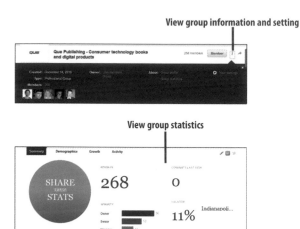

Search a Group

Finding the right information in a popular group can be difficult. Fortunately, LinkedIn enables you to search groups by keyword and other criteria.

1. Click the Search tab on a group page.

2. Enter a search term.

3. Click the Search button to display matching discussions.

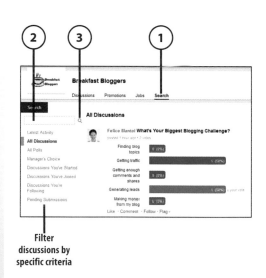

Filter discussions by specific criteria

View Group Members

Viewing a list of group members makes it easy to see if you already know other members of your group. You can also send messages to group members from this page (selectively; don't spam your fellow group members).

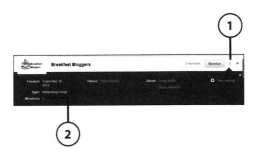

1. Click the *i* icon on a group page.

2. Click the number of members.

3. View of list of group members.

4. Enter search criteria and click the Search button to search for members by name or keyword.

5. Click the See Activity link to view a list of this person's group activity.

6. Click the Send Message link to send this person a message.

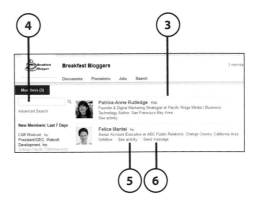

Following and Unfollowing

You automatically follow anyone who is your 1st degree connection. To optionally follow another group member, click the Follow link below that person's photo.

Manage Group Settings

The Settings page enables you to modify the visibility and contact options for that group.

1. Click the *i* icon on a group page.

2. Click the Your Settings link.

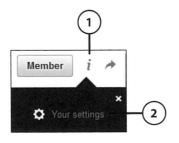

3. Remove the check mark next to the Group Logo check box if you don't want to display this group's logo on your home page.

4. Select the email address where you want LinkedIn to email you group news and updates.

5. Select the Activity check box to receive an email every time someone posts a new discussion.

6. Select the Digest Email check box to receive a daily or weekly email digest of all group activity.

7. Select the Announcements check box to allow the group manager to send you email.

8. Select the Member Messages check box to allow other group members to send you email. (They won't see your personal email address.)

9. Click the Save Changes button.

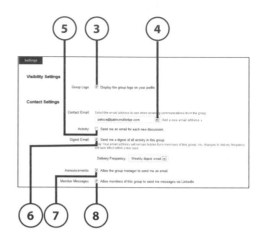

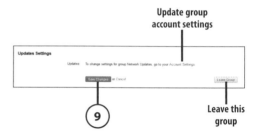

Update group account settings

Leave this group

It's Not All Good

AVOIDING GROUP EMAIL OVERLOAD

Although it's good to keep up with the activity on your favorite groups, your email inbox can quickly become overloaded with messages if you belong to a lot of popular groups. When establishing your preferences on the Settings page, consider carefully which email notifications are really essential and which aren't.

To save time, you can manage all your group digest activity in one place. On the Account & Settings page, go to the Groups, Companies & Applications tab and click the Set Frequency of Group Digest Emails link. Here, you can quickly specify your email preferences for all your groups.

Even if you don't want to receive email notifications, you can keep up with your groups on LinkedIn. Your home page displays group updates, and the Updates page for each group summarizes the latest activity as well.

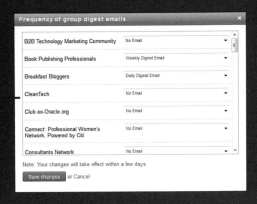

Manage group emails in one place.

Share a Group with Other LinkedIn Users

If you're a member of a particular group you think your connections would also enjoy, let them know about it by sharing it with them.

1. Click the Share button on any group page.

2. Enter your comments about the group you're sharing.

3. Optionally, share in another group.

4. Optionally, share this group individually with one or more LinkedIn connections.

5. Click the Share button.

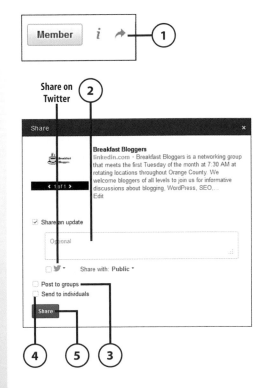

Sharing with Individuals

If you want to share a group with one of your connections, start typing the person's name or email address in the To field and LinkedIn searches for a match. Optionally, you can add more connections or include a customized message.

Leave a Group

If you decide that a group no longer meets your needs or you have to pare down your current group membership to make room for new groups, you can easily leave a group.

To do so, click the Member button in the upper-right corner of any group page. (It becomes the Leave button when you pause over it.) LinkedIn removes you from the group.

Optionally, you can also leave a group by clicking the Leave Group button on a group's Settings page. See the section "Manage Group Settings," earlier in this chapter for more information.

Leave a group

Creating and Managing Your Own Group

Creating your own group is a good way to develop a community for a topic, profession, or interest.

CONSIDERATIONS BEFORE CREATING YOUR OWN GROUP

Before you create a group, consider the following:

- Is there already a similar group on LinkedIn Groups? If so, how will your group differ? What value will you add?

- Is your proposed group an advertisement in disguise? Although many LinkedIn members do benefit from their participation with LinkedIn groups, you need to create a group whose focus is providing value and community to its members. If you don't, your group most likely won't succeed.

- Do you have the time to maintain and support your group? If you don't respond quickly to join requests and keep the activity going with your group, it won't flourish.

Create Your Own Group

Creating a LinkedIn group is easy—managing it and helping it grow is the more difficult part.

1. Select Groups from the Interests menu.

2. Click the Create a Group button.

3. Click the Choose File button to select and upload a logo for your group.

Logo Specifications

Supported formats include PNG, JPEG, and GIF files no larger than 100KB.

4. Select the check box below your logo to confirm that you have a legal right to use this image.

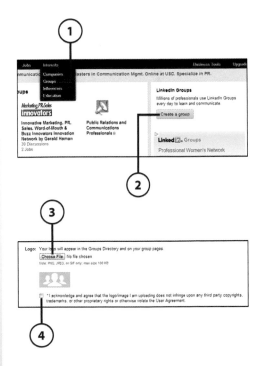

5. Enter a group name.

6. Select a group type. Options include alumni, corporate, conference, networking, nonprofit, professional, or other groups (such as hobby or special interest).

7. Enter a summary of your group. In this text box, indicate your group's focus, goals, and any membership benefits your group might provide for LinkedIn members.

8. In the Description text box, enter more details to display on your group pages.

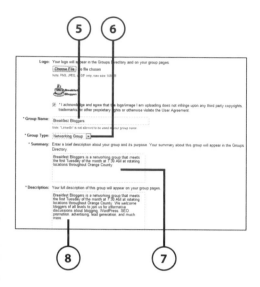

9. If your group has an external website, enter the URL in the Website field.

10. Enter the group owner email. LinkedIn sends all messages about your group to this email address.

11. If you want to approve new group members automatically, select the Auto-Join option button.

12. If you want to approve group membership requests manually, select the Request to Join option button.

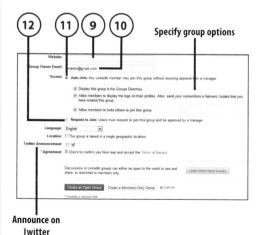

Specify group options

Announce on
Twitter

Approving Group Members

LinkedIn sends a message whenever someone requests to join your group, and you must approve the request manually. This requires extra effort on your part, but it ensures that only qualified people join your group. If your group members work for the same organization, you can preapprove members with a specific email domain.

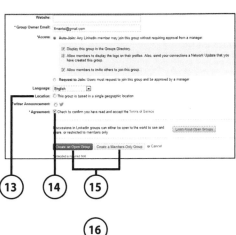

13. If your group is for members who are located in a specific geographic location, select the Location check box and enter the location.

14. If you agree to the Terms of Service, select the check box. The Terms of Service cover your rights to provide LinkedIn with the email addresses of group members and LinkedIn's rights to use the logo you upload.

Skip invitations

15. Click either the Create an Open Group button or the Create a Members-Only Group button to create your group. See the "Open Groups Versus Members-Only Groups" sidebar earlier in this chapter for guidance on which type of group to choose.

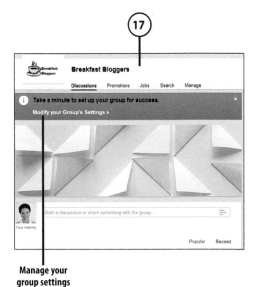

16. Optionally, enter the names of connections you want to invite to your group and click the Send Invitations button.

17. LinkedIn displays your new group.

Manage your
group settings

Manage Your Own Group

Detailed information about LinkedIn's extensive group-management features is beyond the scope of this book. Here's a brief overview of what you can do on your group's Manage tab (visible only to group owners and managers):

- Control the tabs and features you want to include on your group page (Jobs, Promotions, Polls, and so forth)

- Manage member permissions and restrictions, such as who can post what and whether or not you want to moderate submissions

- Moderate flagged content

- Send invitations and announcements

- Add group rules

- Add and manage other group managers

- Preapprove members

- Create subgroups for specific member interests

- Delete your group

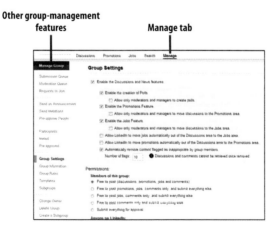

LinkedIn's
Company Page

Follow this
company

View
updates

See who you know
at this company

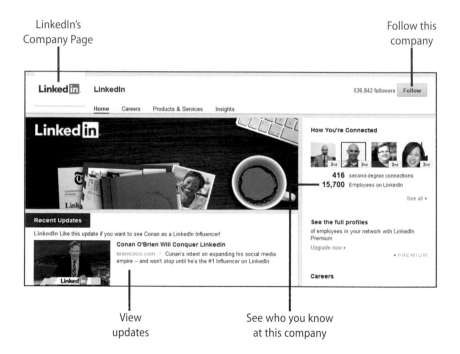

In this chapter, you discover how to search for companies that meet your target criteria and create a LinkedIn Company Page for your own company.

→ Exploring Company Pages

→ Searching for companies

→ Following and unfollowing companies

→ Creating and managing Company Pages

→ Posting updates to your page

Working with Company Pages

LinkedIn Company Pages provide an opportunity for companies to present their products, services, and job openings to LinkedIn's vast audience. In addition, Company Pages offer extensive data that's particularly useful to job seekers, recruiters, and members searching for potential clients and partners.

Exploring LinkedIn Company Pages

LinkedIn Company Pages can include

- Status updates that you can like, share, and comment on

- A Follow button that enables you to follow a company's updates on LinkedIn

- A company description and website URL

- Links to open jobs posted on LinkedIn, if any

- Information about the company's products and services, which you can recommend

- A list of current employees who are in your network or are alumni of the schools you attended

- Company videos

A Company Page updatea

Products and services on a Company Page

Searching for Companies

There are two ways to search for companies on LinkedIn.

Search for Companies by Name

If you know the name of the company you want to find, you can search for it directly.

1. Select Companies from the search menu.

2. Start typing the company name in the search box. As you type, LinkedIn displays potential matches in a drop-down list.

3. Select a company from the list to open its Company Page.

Search for Companies by Specific Criteria

A quick search works well if you know the company you want to find. At times, however, you might want to search for companies that fit target criteria rather than locate a company you already know. For example, you can search for companies by keyword, industry, location, and so forth.

1. Select Companies from the search menu.

2. Enter your search term in the search box.

3. Click the Search button.

4. LinkedIn displays matching companies.

5. Optionally, refine your search selecting criteria in the Search column.

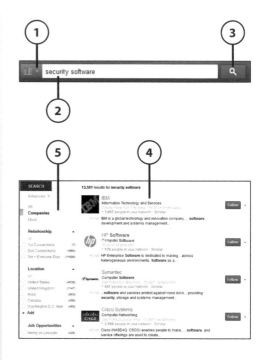

Narrowing Search Results

You can search for companies by location, industry, size, or number of followers. Narrowing search results by displaying only companies with employees in your network or that have job postings on LinkedIn is another option. You don't need to complete all the fields in the Search column, however. In fact, you can generate the best results by starting with your most important criteria and then modifying criteria only if your initial search doesn't yield the desired results.

6. Click a company's name to view its Company Page.

7. Click the Follow button next to a company to follow it.

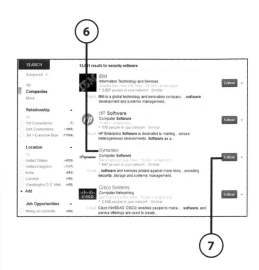

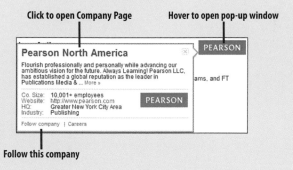

>>>Go Further

ACCESSING COMPANY PAGES FROM LINKEDIN PROFILES

Hover your mouse over a company name or logo on a member's profile to display a pop-up window with additional company information. If no pop-up displays, a Company Page doesn't exist yet.

Following and Unfollowing Companies

As you learned earlier in this chapter, you can follow a company by

- Clicking the Follow button in the upper-right corner of its Company Page
- Clicking the Follow button next to a company's name in search results
- Clicking the Follow link in a company pop-up window that you access from someone's profile

When you follow a company on LinkedIn, its updates display on your home page.

Following companies is a good way to keep up with the latest news in your own company (particularly if you work for a large corporation) as well as discover new developments at companies you would like to work for or pursue as clients. You can follow up to 1,000 companies on LinkedIn.

Unfollow a Company

If a company no longer interests you or you followed it by mistake, you can unfollow it.

1. Select Companies from the Interests menu.

2. LinkedIn displays a list of the companies you're following.

3. Click the Stop Following link below the company you no longer want to follow.

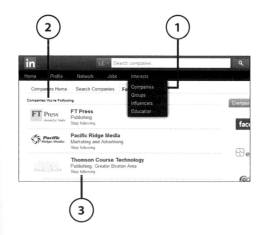

Alternative Way to Unfollow a Company

If you're already viewing the Company Page of a company you want to unfollow, click the Following button in the upper-right corner to unfollow it. (The button acts as a toggle.)

Creating and Managing a Company Page

If your company doesn't already have a Company Page, you can create one. Be aware that you must have the authority to create a page on behalf of a company (an important consideration if you work for a larger organization).

In addition, you must meet the following requirements to create a Company Page:

- You're listed as an employee for this company in the Experience section of your profile.

- You have a company email address using the domain of the company you want to add. For example, to add the Really Great Company at www.reallygreatcompany.com, you must have an email address for this company such as anne@reallygreatcompany.com. You can't use a Gmail or Yahoo! Mail address to register a company.

- Your profile strength must be either Intermediate or All-Star.

- You have at least several connections.

Promote Your Small Business with a Company Page

Company Pages aren't just for large corporations. If you own a small business, even a one-person business, creating a page can help you gain visibility on LinkedIn.

It's Not All Good

COMPANY PAGES AREN'T ADVERTISEMENTS

Remember, however, that a Company Page isn't an advertisement in disguise. Stick to the facts and avoid hype. Read other pages in your industry before creating your own to understand what is and isn't appropriate.

Create a Company Page

1. Select Companies from the Interests menu.

2. Click the Add a Company link.

3. Enter your company name and email address at that company.

4. Select the check box to verify that you have the right to create this page.

5. Click the Continue button.

6. Follow the prompts LinkedIn provides to create your Company Page and confirm your identity. This process varies based on your company, your email address, and your LinkedIn account. You must verify your identity and your company before LinkedIn allows you to finish your page.

7. The Overview tab for your Company Page opens, prompting you to add a description of your company.

8. If you want to add another administrator to your page, start typing this person's name and select it from the drop-down list. You can give admin rights only to your 1st degree connection.

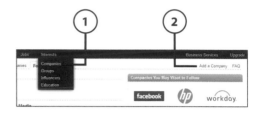

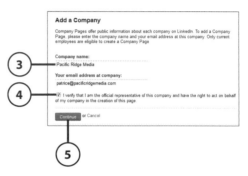

Company Page Administrators

A LinkedIn Company Page administrator can edit Company Page content, post updates, add products and services, and add other admins. LinkedIn automatically gives the person who creates a Company Page admin rights and this person can, optionally, add more admins. You should select your page admins carefully; these people have the power to control the appearance and reputation of your company on LinkedIn.

9. Add images for your company, including a header image, standard logo, and square logo.

Image Size Requirements

You can upload PNG, JPG, or GIF images that are no larger than 2MB. Your company's main image must be 646×220 pixels or larger. LinkedIn resizes your standard logo to 100×60 pixels and your square logo to 50×50 pixels.

10. Enter company keywords in the Company Specialties field. This is a good place to list services or topics related to your business, such as digital marketing, copywriting, project management training, small business accounting, and so forth.

11. If you have a LinkedIn group, start typing its name in the Featured Groups field and select it from the drop-down menu.

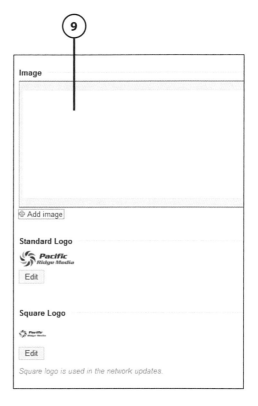

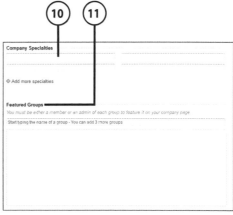

12. Enter basic company information by completing the fields in the boxes on the right side of the page, including Company Type, Company Size, Company Website URL, Company Locations, and so forth.

13. Optionally, click the Products & Services tab if you want to add information about your company's products and services.

Listing Products & Services

Maximizing the potential of the Products & Services tab is a great promotional tool for most companies. For each item you list on this page, you can include a detailed description, image, YouTube video, special promotion, and link for more information. Your followers can also recommend your products and services to other LinkedIn members.

14. Click the Publish button to save changes and publish your Company Page.

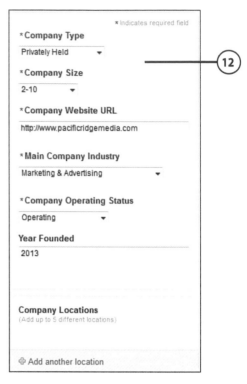

Add products and services to your page

WHAT HAPPENS NEXT?

After you create your Company Page, you should let your network know of its existence and encourage your connections and employees to follow your page. To keep your page active, be sure to update content regularly by posting updates and adding any new products or services. LinkedIn provides a direct URL to your Company Page, such as www.linkedin.com/company/linkedin, that you can bookmark for your convenience. You can also return to your page by selecting Companies from the Interests menu and clicking your company name in the list of companies you're following.

Post an Update to a Company Page

LinkedIn enables you to share company news with your followers in the Share an Update box on your Company Page. You can share a basic text update of up to 600 characters; a link title, description, and optional photo; or an external file you attach.

See the section "Sharing Updates," in Chapter 5, "Managing and Updating Your Profile," for more details about sharing updates. Company Page updates are similar to the personal updates you post on LinkedIn.

1. While logged into LinkedIn, navigate to your Company Page, such as www.linkedin.com/company/linkedin.

2. In the Share an Update box, enter your update, such as a text update or URL.

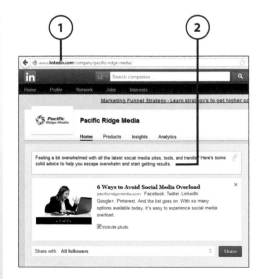

3. Optionally, click the Attach a File icon to attach an external file such as an image.

4. By default LinkedIn shares your update with all your followers. Optionally, you can select Targeted Audience to narrow your audience by specific criteria.

Consider Sponsored Updates

If you want to get more visibility for your company updates, consider LinkedIn's Sponsored Updates program. See Chapter 16, "Advertising on LinkedIn," for more information.

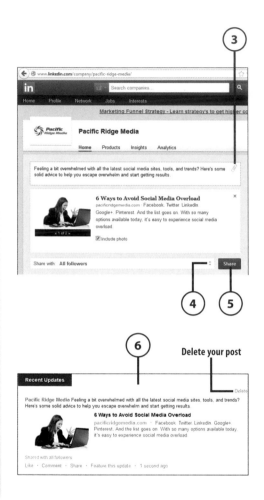

5. Click the Share button.

6. LinkedIn displays your update on your Company Page, which your followers can like, share, or comment on.

Edit a Company Page

If you're an authorized Company Page admin, you can add, edit, and delete page content.

See the "Create a Company Page" section earlier in this chapter for more information about the data you can enter for a company.

1. While logged into LinkedIn, navigate to your Company Page, such as www.linkedin.com/company/linkedin.

2. Click the Edit button.

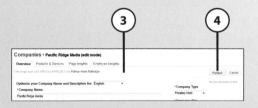

3. Make your page changes.

4. Click the Publish button to update and save your Company Page.

>>>Go Further

MANAGING YOUR COMPANY PAGE

Here are some tips for managing your Company Page as it grows:

- View page statistics by clicking the Analytics tab on your Company Page. On this tab, you can view detailed information about your updates, followers, reach, and engagement.

- LinkedIn members can associate themselves with your company and its page when they specify an employer on their profiles. If you find someone associated with your company who isn't an actual employee, you can request that LinkedIn remove this person at http://help.linkedin.com/app/ask/path/rmfcp.

- Jobs you post through LinkedIn Jobs display on the Careers tab of your Company Page. If you don't have posted jobs, LinkedIn members won't see this tab. Optionally, you can upgrade to a Gold or Silver Career Page (http://business.linkedin.com/talent-solutions/products/career-pages.html), which enables you to add clickable banners, customized content, and videos to your Careers tab. This program is most suited to larger companies with many open positions.

- Although you can't delete a Company Page yourself, you can ask LinkedIn to do so for you at http://help.linkedin.com/app/ask/path/cprr. Your page must have fewer than five employees associated with it to request deletion.

Ad that's part
of an ad square

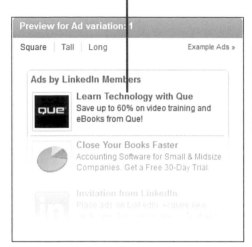

Long ad

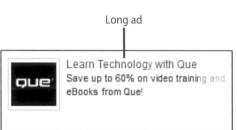

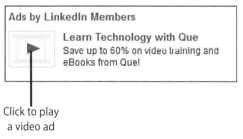

Click to play
a video ad

The video plays directly
on the LinkedIn page

In this chapter, you explore LinkedIn advertising programs, including LinkedIn Ads and Sponsored Posts.

→ Creating an ad
→ Sponsoring an update
→ Managing your ads

16

Advertising on LinkedIn

LinkedIn offers two low-cost advertising options: LinkedIn Ads and Sponsored Updates. LinkedIn Ads is a text-based advertising program that focuses on reaching the site's highly targeted demographics with ads placed on the home page and member profiles. Sponsored Updates enable you to display selected updates from your LinkedIn Company Page on the feeds of targeted LinkedIn members rather than just on your Company Page itself.

Working with LinkedIn Ads

LinkedIn Ads enables businesses with advertising budgets as low as $10 per day to display text ads on LinkedIn. The LinkedIn Ads program is a self-service advertising option, similar to Google AdWords. You enter your ad online and pay for it with a credit card. LinkedIn ads display in different formats depending on where they are placed on the site.

>>>*Go Further*

LINKEDIN ADS TIPS

Here are some tips for creating ads that generate results:

- **Because a text ad contains so few words, make every word count**—Your first effort will most likely contain too many words. Keep revising until you can communicate your message effectively within the ad length limitations.

- **Focus on a call to action**—You need to pique the interest of your target audience and encourage them to click your ad for more information.

- **Check your grammar and spelling**—Errors make your ad look unprofessional and reduce your click-through rate.

- **Verify that your URL works**—Even worse than grammar and spelling errors is a URL that doesn't work or leads to the wrong place.

- **Avoid using all capitalization in your ad**—Use title case for your headline and sentence case for your remaining ad.

- **Avoid ad content and topics that violate LinkedIn Ads Guidelines**—This includes ads for alcohol, tobacco, drugs, gambling, firearms, adult products, dating services, or multilevel marketing programs. Click the Advertising Guidelines link at the bottom of any LinkedIn Ads page to view the complete guidelines.

Create a LinkedIn Ad

It takes only a few minutes to set up an ad, but it's a good idea to spend a bit more time analyzing your approach, content, and goals if you want to succeed.

1. On the bottom menu, click the Advertising link.

2. Click the Start Now button.

3. Click the Create an Ad button.

4. Enter a descriptive name for your ad. This doesn't appear on your ad; it's for your reference only.

5. Select a media type: Basic (text and images) or Video. In this example, you create a basic ad.

Video Ads

A video ad enables you to create a link to a YouTube video of less than 120 seconds that people can play directly on the LinkedIn website.

6. Select an ad destination—either a web page or a page on LinkedIn, such as your LinkedIn Company Page.

7. Click the Add Image link to display an image on your ad.

Image Requirements

Images must be in PNG, JPEG, or GIF format and no more than 2MB in size. Images display as a 50×50 pixel square only on ads in locations that support an ad thumbnail.

Manage existing ads

Learn more about LinkedIn Ads

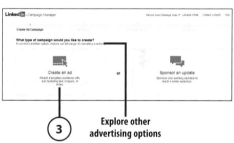

Explore other advertising options

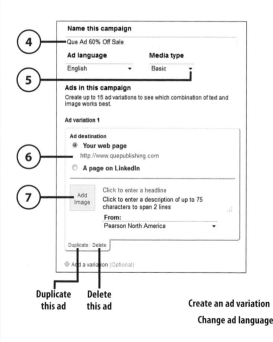

Duplicate this ad

Delete this ad

Create an ad variation

Change ad language

8. Enter a headline of up to 25 characters.

Headline Tips

Your headline is what draws members to your ad. Make it memorable and clear.

9. Enter your ad text of up to 75 characters, which can span two lines.

10. Select a profile link from the drop-down list. You can display either your personal LinkedIn profile or a LinkedIn Company Page.

Creating Multiple Versions

If you want to create multiple variations of your ad, click the Add a Variation link and complete the new ad. For example, you could change the headline or wording slightly to see which ad performs better. To save time, click the Duplicate link in your first ad to duplicate and then modify it. You can create up to 15 ad variations.

11. Preview your ad and make any necessary changes before proceeding.

12. Click Next to open the Targeting page.

Change ad language

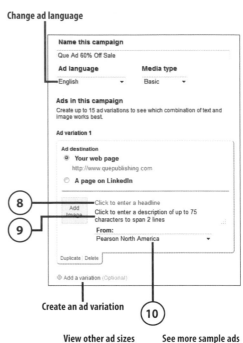

Create an ad variation

View other ad sizes   See more sample ads

View ad tips

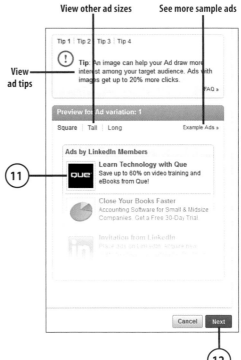

13. Select one or more locations for your ad.

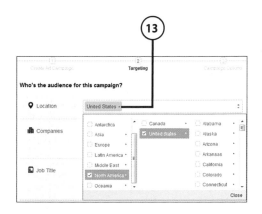

Targeting Metro Areas

In many locations, you can narrow your target audience to a specific metro area, such as the San Francisco Bay Area or the Greater New York City Area.

14. Optionally, target your ad by company, industry, or company size.

15. Optionally, target your ad to a specific job title, category, or function.

Finding Additional Target Options

Click the More Target Options link to apply additional filters for your ad. For example, you can target your ad by school, skills, LinkedIn group membership, gender, or age.

16. If you want to display your ad on LinkedIn partner sites as well as LinkedIn.com, select the Also Reach LinkedIn Members on Other Websites Through the LinkedIn Audience Network check box.

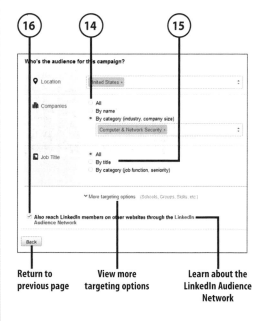

Return to previous page

View more targeting options

Learn about the LinkedIn Audience Network

17. View the Audience section field to see the effects of narrowing your audience. You can modify your criteria if the summary results don't match the audience size you want to reach.

Analyzing Your Target Audience

Before continuing to the next page, review your estimated target audience carefully. Consider who you want to reach and why. Is your estimated target audience too big or too small? Sometimes a small target audience can yield better results, but other times it just doesn't give you enough reach.

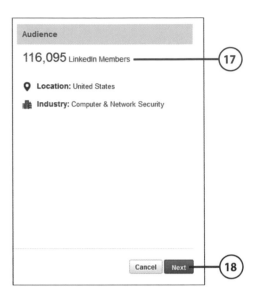

18. Click the Next button to open the Campaign Options page.

19. Specify whether you want to pay when someone clicks on your ad (CPC) or every time LinkedIn displays your ad. See the section "Understanding How to Pay for LinkedIn Ads," for more information.

20. Enter the amount of money you're willing to spend each day in the Daily Budget field. LinkedIn continues to display your ad until you reach this limit. The minimum you can enter is $10.

21. Specify whether you want to show your campaign continuously or until a specified date. It's best to run a long-term campaign unless you're marketing something that's time-sensitive, such as an event.

22. Select the Turn on Lead Collection for This Campaign check box if you want to display a button

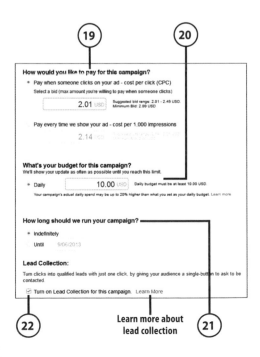

Learn more about lead collection

that people can click to request contact from your organization.

23. Click the Save Changes button to open the Billing Information page.

24. Enter your personal and credit card information in the specified fields.

25. Click the Review Order button to review your order and place your ad.

What Happens Next?

LinkedIn charges your credit card $5 and credits this amount to your LinkedIn Ads account. After receiving approval from LinkedIn that your ad meets its advertising guidelines, the ad begins to appear on the LinkedIn site based on the targeted criteria you specify.

Review your choices

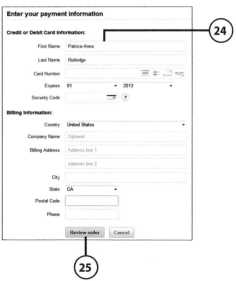

UNDERSTANDING HOW TO PAY FOR LINKEDIN ADS

LinkedIn offers two options for paying for your ads. It's important to understand the difference between these options before making your selection, particularly if you're new to online advertising.

The first option—paying when someone clicks your ad—is referred to as cost per click (CPC) advertising. When you choose a CPC advertising model, you pay only when someone clicks your ad. Enter the maximum amount you're willing to pay for each click. You might pay less per click depending on demand, but you won't pay more than this amount. LinkedIn displays a suggested range based on the current bids of other advertisers, but you can enter any amount you want that meets or exceeds the minimum of $2.

The second option enables you to pay every time LinkedIn displays your ad. This method is referred to as CPM advertising, which stands for cost per mille (thousand) views. When you choose a CPM advertising model, you pay a fixed amount for every 1,000 ad views regardless of how many clicks it receives. LinkedIn displays a suggested range based on the current bids of other advertisers, but you can enter any amount you want that meets or exceeds the minimum of $2.

Working with Sponsored Updates

If you have a LinkedIn Company page and post status updates, the Sponsored Updates advertising program enables you to display selected updates on the feeds of targeted LinkedIn members even if they don't read your Company Page. See Chapter 15, "Working with Company Pages," for more information on creating a page and posting updates.

Sponsor an Update

Sponsoring an update is a simple task. What's more difficult is the strategy behind this: choosing the best update to sponsor and the best audience to target.

1. On the bottom menu, click the Advertising link.

2. Click the Start Now button.

3. Click the Sponsor an Update button.

A LinkedIn Company Page Is Required

When you click the Sponsor an Update button, LinkedIn displays a warning message if you don't already have a Company Page with updates. You can't continue until you create a page.

4. Enter a name for your campaign.

5. Select a campaign language.

6. Select a Company Page from the drop-down list.

7. Select the check box next to the update you want to sponsor.

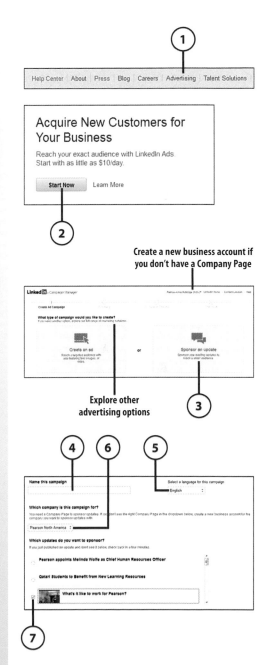

① Help Center About Press Blog Careers Advertising Talent Solutions

Acquire New Customers for Your Business

Reach your exact audience with LinkedIn Ads. Start with as little as $10/day.

Start Now   Learn More

②

Create a new business account if you don't have a Company Page

③

Explore other advertising options

④ ⑥ ⑤

⑦

8. Preview the selected update.

9. Click Next.

10. Select one or more locations for your ad.

11. Optionally, target your ad by company, industry, or company size.

12. Optionally, target your ad to a specific job title, category, or function.

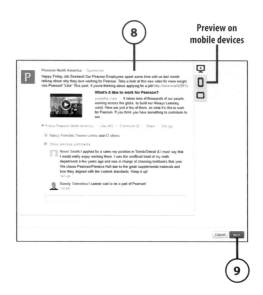

Preview on mobile devices

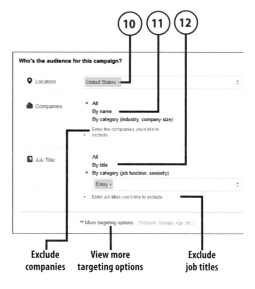

Exclude companies

View more targeting options

Exclude job titles

13. Click Next.

14. Specify whether you want to pay when someone clicks on your ad (CPC) or every time LinkedIn displays your ad. See the section "Understanding How to Pay for LinkedIn Ads," earlier in this chapter for more information.

Social Actions Are Free

LinkedIn doesn't charge for social actions, such as likes, comments, shares, or follows.

---

15. Enter the amount of money you're willing to spend each day or provide a total budget. LinkedIn continues to display your ad until you reach this limit. The minimum you can enter is $10.

16. Specify whether you want to show your campaign continuously or until a specified date. It's best to run a long-term campaign unless you're marketing something that's time-sensitive, such as an event.

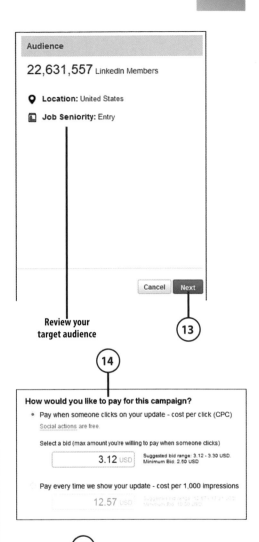

17. Click the Save Changes button to open the Billing Information page.

18. Enter your personal and credit card information in the specified fields.

19. Click the Review Order button to review your order and place your ad.

What Happens Next?

As soon as LinkedIn verifies your billing information, your sponsored updates start running immediately.

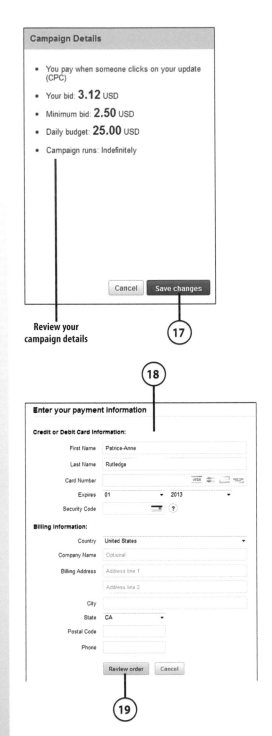

Campaign Details

- You pay when someone clicks on your update (CPC)
- Your bid: **3.12** USD
- Minimum bid: **2.50** USD
- Daily budget: **25.00** USD
- Campaign runs: Indefinitely

Cancel   Save changes

Review your campaign details

17

18

Enter your payment information

Credit or Debit Card Information:

First Name   Patrice-Anne
Last Name   Rutledge
Card Number
Expires   01   2013
Security Code

Billing Information:

Country   United States
Company Name   Optional
Billing Address   Address line 1
                  Address line 2
City
State   CA
Postal Code
Phone

Review order   Cancel

19

>>>Go Further

MANAGING YOUR LINKEDIN ADS

To manage your ads and view reports of your results, go to www.linkedin.com/ads/home.

The LinkedIn Ads Dashboard has four tabs:

- **Campaigns**—View a summary of your results for each ad, such as your status, daily budget, ad clicks, impressions, click-through rate (CTR), average CPC, and total spent. You can also click an ad name for more details, turn your ads on and off the LinkedIn network, and hide them from this tab.

What's CTR?

CTR is a common online advertising term that stands for *click-through rate*. Your CTR tells you the percentage of people who clicked your ad. Remember, however, that some people don't immediately click links in ads; they do, however, later visit website links that are shown in ads.

- **Leads**—View a list of your leads, which you can filter by date, contact status, and campaign.

- **Reporting**—View reports that detail your impressions and clicks over specific time periods. You can download the reports in a CSV (comma-separated values) format to import into applications such as Microsoft Excel.

- **Settings**—Give permission to LinkedIn to contact you about ad problems, campaigns that are ending, or campaign optimization opportunities.

The LinkedIn Ads
Dashboard is empty until   Start a new
your ads start running   campaign

Index

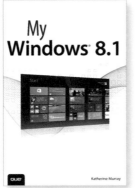

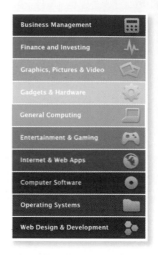

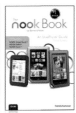